DICTIONARY OF
MULTIMEDIA

Titles in the series

(see back of this book for full title list and information request form)

Also Available

Workbooks for teachers and students of specialist English:

DICTIONARY OF
MULTIMEDIA

Editor

S.M.H. Collin

PETER COLLIN PUBLISHING

First published in Great Britain 1995

published by
Peter Collin Publishing Ltd
1 Cambridge Road, Teddington, Middlesex, TW11 8DT

British Library Cataloguing in Publication Data

A Catalogue record for this book is available from the British Library

ISBN 0-948549-69-6

Text computer typeset by PCP
Printed and bound in Great Britain by
Butler & Tanner Ltd, Frome and London

Cover design by Gary Weston

PREFACE

Multimedia is one of the most exciting areas of computing, but it is packed with jargon and complex technical terms. The aim of this dictionary is to explain the terms that are used in multimedia. It is aimed at anyone who is interested in the subject, from developers to users, and is packed with over 3,000 terms.

All terms are clearly and simply defined, and screen-shots from software are included to show various types of software. At the back of the book is an appendix with tables of useful data.

I have tried to include all the relevant technical terms for the standards that define the audio, video and images used in multimedia. Standards are continuously changing but I have included all the current and forthcoming terms that will be in use for the next few years. I have also included details of the major products within various categories.

I hope that you find this dictionary useful and that it helps you get the most from multimedia.

Numbers

2D
object in a graphic image that has only the appearance of width and height, not depth, so does not look like a solid object

3D
object in a graphic image that has the appearance of width, height and depth and so looks like a solid object
see also
RENDER

3DO™
hardware platform with a built-in CD-ROM drive, RISC-based processor, graphics adapter and sound generator

6 degrees of freedom
(in virtual reality) description of the movements and vision that a user can interpret: normally three visual dimensions together with movement

8-bit
data that is transferred eight bits at a time along eight parallel conductors; in a processor this refers to its ability to manipulate numbers that are eight bits long that can represent numbers up to 256

8-bit sample
single sample of an analogue signal which is stored as an 8-bit digital number,

meaning that there are 256 possible levels
see also
16-BIT SAMPLE

16-bit

data that is transferred sixteen bits at a time along sixteen parallel conductors; in a processor this refers to its ability to manipulate numbers that are sixteen bits long representing numbers up to 65,536

16-bit sample

single sample of an analog signal which is stored as a 16-bit digital number, meaning that there are 65,536 possible levels; NOTE: a "16-bit sound card" can also mean that it generates 8-bit samples, but fits into a 16-bit expansion slot
see also
8-BIT SAMPLE

32-bit

data that is transferred thirty-two bits at a time along thrity-two parallel conductors; in a processor this refers to its ability to manipulate numbers that are thrity-two bits long

8086, 80286, 80386, 80486

family of processors developed by Intel that can manipulate 8, 16, and 32-bit numbers; used in IBM-PC compatible computers
for more details, see
INTEL

68000, 68020, 68030, 68040

family of processors developed by Motorola that can maniipulate 16 and 32-bit numbers; used in the Apple Macintosh range of computers
for more details, see
MOTOROLA, APPLE

Aa

A to D converter *or* A/D converter
ANALOG TO DIGITAL CONVERTER
device used to convert an analog input to a digital output form which can be understood by a computer or other digital circuit such as a digital signal processor
compare with
D/A CONVERTER

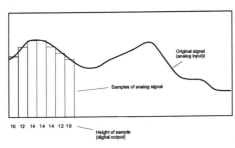

Analog to digital conversion

About...
(in the SAA CUA front-end) menu selection that tells you who developed the program and gives copyright information

AB roll
two video or music segments that are synchronized so that one fades as the second starts

absolute time

(in CD DA) length of time that an audio disc has been playing

acceleration time

time taken for a disk drive to spin a disk to the correct speed, from rest

accelerator

see
ACCELERATOR KEY

accelerator board *or* card

circuit board that carries a faster version of the processor in a computer; adding an accelerator card to your computer makes it run faster

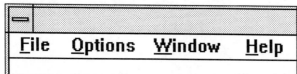

within Windows, press Alt with the underlined accelerator key

accelerator key

combination of keys that, when pressed together, carry out a function that would otherwise have to be selected from a menu using a mouse; for example, to save a document, either select Save from the File menu or press Alt-S

access

being allowed to use a computer and read or alter files stored in it (this is usually controlled by a security device such as a password)

access controller

(in CD-i) electronic device that transfers image data to the video controller

access time

(i) total time which a storage device takes between the moment the data is requested and the data being returned; (ii) length of time required to find a file or program, either in main memory or a secondary memory source; CD-ROM drives have a normal access time of 400msec for a single speed and 300msec for a double-speed drive, whilst a hard disk has an access time of around 25msec

accessory

extra, add-on device (such as a mouse or printer) which is attached to or used with a computer

4

achromatic colour

(grey) colour within the range between black and white displayed by a graphics adapter

Acorn Computers

developersof the BBC micro and the Archimedes computer

acoustic panel

sound-proofed panel placed around a device to reduce noise

acoustic coupler

device that connects to a telephone handset, converting binary computer data into sound signals to allow data to be transmitted down a telephone line; the acoustic coupler also converts back from sound signals to digital signals when receiving messages; it is basically the same as a modem but uses a handset on which a loudspeaker is placed to send the signals rather than direct connection to the phone line. One major advantage of an acoustic coupler is that it is portable, and clips over both ends of a normal telephone handset; it can be used even in a public phone booth

acoustics

study of sound or the characteristics of a sound

acquisition

accepting or capturing or collecting information

ACR

AUDIO CASSETTE RECORDER

ACR interface

interface which allows a cassette recorder to be linked to a computer

Acrobat™

file format (developed by Adobe Systems) that describes a graphics image and allows the same image.file to be displayed on different hardware; for example, if you use Acrobat on a Macintosh and a PC, you can easily exchange graphics files

acronym

abbreviation, formed from various letters, which makes up a word which can be pronounced; for example, GUI is an acronym of graphical user interface and is pronounced 'gooey'

action

(in an SAA CUA front-end) user event, such as pressing a special key, that moves the cursor to the action or menu bar at the top of the screen

action bar

(in an SAA CUA front-end) top line of the screen that displays the menu names

action bar pull-down

(in an SAA CUA front-end) standard that defines what happens when a user moves the cursor to a particular menu name on the action bar: the full menu is displayed below the menu name

action code

(in an SAA CUA front-end) single letter associated with a particular menu option to speed up selection; when the letter action code is pressed, the menu option is selected; for example, in Windows, the convention is F for the file menu, E for the edit menu, and H for the help menu

action cycle

complete set of actions involved in one operation (including reading data, processing, storing results, etc.)

action list

(in an SAA CUA front-end) list of choices

action message

message displayed to inform the user that an action or input is required

action-object

(in an SAA CUA front-end) object to which a user specifies an action should be applied

activated

(in an authoring tool or programming language) button or field in a screen layout that has a script attached to it; the script is executed when the user clicks on the button; NOTE: if the button or field is not activated, it is normally displayed greyed out and does not respond if a user selects it

active matrix liquid crystal display

way of making liquid crystal displays (for laptop computer screens) in which each pixel is controlled by its own transistor

active menu
menu selection currently displayed below a menu bar

active region
area on a screen that will start an action or has been defined as a hotspot

active window
(i) area of display screen in which you are currently working; (ii) (in a GUI or SAA CUA front-end), the window that is currently the focus of cursor movements and screen displays
see also
WINDOW

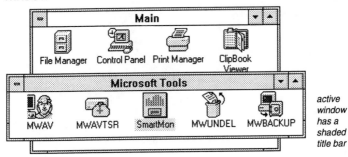

active window has a shaded title bar

A/D *or* A to D
ANALOG TO DIGITAL

adapter
device that allows two or more incompatible devices to be connected together so that they can transfer data

adapter card
interface card (that plugs into an expansion slot in a computer) that allows incompatible devices to communicate; for example, a display adapter allows a computer to display text and images on a monitor

adaptive interframe transform coding
class of compression algorithms commonly used with video signals to reduce the data transmission rate

adaptive differential pulse-code modulation (ADPCM)
CCITT standard that defines a method of converting a voice or analog signal into a compressed digital signal

ADB™
APPLE DESKTOP BUS

serial bus built into Apple Macintosh computers that allows low-speed devices, such as the keyboard and mouse, to communicate with the processor

ADC
ANALOG TO DIGITAL CONVERSION

converting an analog input to a digital output form, that can be understood by a computer

ADC
ANALOG TO DIGITAL CONVERTOR

electronic device that converts an analog input signal to a digital output form, that can be used by a computer

A/D converter
see
ANALOG TO DIGITAL CONVERTER

address
(i) number allowing a central processing unit to reference a physical location in a storage medium in a computer system; (ii) unique number that identifies a device on a network

address bus
physical connection that carries the address data in parallel form from the central processing unit to external devices

address mapping
(in a virtual memory system) virtual address that is translated to a real address
see also
VIRTUAL MEMORY

address space
total number of possible locations that can be directly addressed by the program or CPU

addressable cursor
cursor which can be programmed to be placed in a certain position

addressable point
any point or pixel in a graphics system that can be directly addressed and controlled

AdLib™

type of sound card for the PC with basic sound playback and MIDI functions

Adobe™

software company that has developed products including Acrobat, ATM, and PostScript

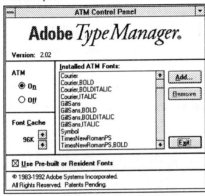

Adobe Type Manager (ATM)

Adobe Type Manager *or* ATM™

software technology for describing scalable fonts - most commonly used with Apple System 7 and Microsoft Windows to provide fonts that can be scaled to almost any point size, and printed on almost any printer

ADPCM

ADAPTIVE DIFFERENTIAL PULSE-CODE MODULATION
CCITT standard that defines a method of converting a voice or analog signal into a compressed digital signal
see also
LEVEL A, LEVEL B, LEVEL C

advanced interactive executive

see
AIX

aerial perspective

view of a three-dimensional landscape as if the viewer is above the scene

AFP

APPLETALK FILING PROTOCOL™
protocol used to communicate between workstations and servers in a network of Apple Macintosh computers

afterglow

see
PERSISTENCE

agent

software that carries out a task automatically, for example running a query on a database every hour

aiming symbol *or* field

symbol displayed on screen which defines the area in which a light-pen can be detected

airbrush

(in graphics software) a painting tool that creates a diffuse pattern of dots, like an mechanical airbrush

air gap

narrow gap between a recording or playback head and the magnetic medium

AIX™

ADVANCED INTERACTIVE EXECUTIVE
version of UNIX developed by IBM to run on its range of PCs, minicomputers and mainframes

alert box

dialog box displayed with a sound that warns a user of the implications of the user's actions

algorithm

mathematical formula that is used to solve a problem

alias

(i) alternative name for something; often used to provide a new keystroke to access a menu item; (ii) undesirable value within a digital sample - often because a very high input signal has exceeded the limits of the converter and is wrongly represented as a very low value

align

(i) to make sure that the characters to be printed are spaced and levelled correctly, either vertically or horizontally; (ii) to arrange numbers into a column with all figures lined up against the right hand side (right-aligned) or the left-hand side (left-aligned); (iii) to ensure that a read/write head is correctly positioned over the recording medium

align text

(in a word-processor) to add spaces between words in a line to make sure that the line of text fills the whole line
see also
JUSTIFY

all points addressable (APA) mode

graphics mode in which each pixel can be individually addressed and its colour and attributes defined

ALPHA™

processor chip developed by Digital Equipment Corporation; the ALPHA chip is a 64-bit RISC processor

alpha test

first working attempt of a computer product

alpha channel

(i) video channel; often used to hold mattes; (ii) (in 32-bit graphics systems) the top eight bits of a pixel word that define the properties of a pixel; the lower 24 bits define the pixel's colour
see also
MATTE

alphageometric

(set of codes) that instruct a teletext terminal to display various graphics patterns or characters

alphamosaic

(character set) used in teletext to provide alphanumeric and graphics characters

alphanumeric characters *or* alphanumerics

roman letters and arabic numerals (and other signs such as punctuation marks)

alphasort

to sort data into alphabetical order

Alt key

special key on a PC's keyboard used to activate special functions in an application; the Alt key has become the standard method of activating a menu bar in any software running on a PC; for example, Alt-F normally displays the

File menu of a program, Alt-X normally exits the program

AM
AMPLITUDE MODULATION

ambient noise
normal background noise that is present all the time; normally given a reference pressure level of 0.00002 pascal in SI units

American National Standards Institute (ANSI)
organization which specifies computer and software standards, including those of high-level programming languages

American Standard Code for Information Interchange (ASCII)
code which represents alphanumeric characters using a standard set of binary codes

Amiga™
range of personal computers developed by Commodore. COMMENT: Amiga computers are based on the Motorolla 68000 range of CPUs and are not normally IBM PC compatible without add-on hardware or software

amplification
the ratio of the output signal strength compared to the input signal strength

amplifier
electronic circuit that magnifies the power of a signal

amplify
to magnify the power of a signal or amplitude

amplitude
strength or size of a signal

amplitude modulation (AM)
method of carrying data by varying the size of a carrier signal (of fixed frequency) according to the data
compare with
FREQUENCY MODULATION

amplitude quantization
conversion of an analog signal to a numerical representation

analog *or* analogue

representation and measurement of numerical data by continuously variable physical quantities, such as the size of electrical voltages
compare with
DIGITAL

analog channel

communications line that carries analog signals such as speech

analog data

data that is represented as a continuously variable signal; speech is a form of analog data

analog display

display or monitor that can display an infinite range of colours or shades of grey (unlike digital displays that can only display a finite range of colours); VGA monitors are a form of analog display

analog input card

all circuitry on one PCB required for amplifying and converting analog input signals to a digital form

analog monitor

display screen that uses a continuously variable input signal to control the colours display so it can display a near infinite range of colours; the video monitor accepts analog signals from the computer (digital to analog conversion is performed in the video display board). The monitor may accept only a narrow range of display resolutions; for example, a monitor might only be able to display VGA or VGA and Super VGA, or it may accept a wide range of signals including TV
See also
MULTI-FREQUENCY MONITOR, RGB MONITOR.

analog output card

all circuitry on one PCB required to convert digital output data from a computer to an analog form

analog recording

storing signals in their natural form without conversion to digital form

analog signal

continuously varying signal

analog to digital (A to D *or* A/D)
(changing a signal) from an analog form to a digitally coded form

analog to digital converter (ADC *or* A to D converter)
device used to convert an analog input signal to a digital output form, which can be understood by a computer or other digital circuit such as a digital signal processor
compare with
DIGITAL TO ANALOG CONVERTER

analog to digital conversion (ADC)
converting an analog signal into a digital form that can be understood by a computer

anamorphic lens
optical lens that changes the horizontal perspective of an image

AND
logical function whose output is true if both inputs are true

anechoic chamber
perfectly quiet room in which sound or radio waves do not reflect off the walls

angled line
line with three or more points (such as a zig-zag)

animated graphics
images that move on the screen

animation
creating the illusion of movement by displaying a series of slightly different images on screen; the images are displayed very rapidly to give the effect of smooth movement

animation software
software that allows a user to create and manipulate a series of images so that when played back they give the effect of movement

ANSI
AMERICAN NATIONAL STANDARDS INSTITUTE
organization which specifies computer and software standards, including those of high-level programming languages

ANSI driver

(in a PC) small resident software program that interprets ANSI screen control codes and controls the screen appropriately

ANSI escape sequence

sequence of ANSI screen control characters that controls the colours and attributes of text on screen; the sequence must begin with the ASCII character Esc (ASCII 27) and the character '[' (ASCII 91)

ANSI screen control

standard codes developed by ANSI that control how colours and simple graphics are displayed on a computer screen

anti-aliasing

(i) method of reducing the effects of jagged edges in graphics by using shades of grey to blend in along edges and make angled lines appear smooth; (ii) filter used to correct sampling errors (aliases) due to a very high or low input signal

anti-virus program

software program that looks for virus software on a computer and destroys it before it can damage data or files

APA

ALL POINTS ADDRESSABLE

aperture mask

metal sheet with holes in colour monitors, used to keep the red, green and blue beams separate

API

APPLICATION PROGRAMMING INTERFACE

set of standard program functions and commands that allow any programmer to interface a program with another application

Apple Computer Corporation™

company (formed in 1975) which has developed a range of personal computers including the Apple II, Lisa and, more recently, the Macintosh in both desktop and laptop forms

Apple Desktop Bus (ADB)™

serial bus built into Apple Macintosh computers that allows low-speed devices, such as the keyboard and mouse, to communicate with the processor

Apple file exchange™

software program that runs on an Apple Macintosh computer allowing it to read disks from a PC

Apple filing protocol (AFP) ™

method of storing files on a network server so that they can be accessed from an Apple Macintosh computer

Apple Key

special key on the keyboard of an Apple Macintosh that, when pressed with another key, provides a short cut to a menu selection

Apple Mac *or* Apple Macintosh™

range of personal computers developed by Apple that has a graphical user interface and uses the 68000 family of processors

AppleScript

(on an Apple Macintosh) script language built into the System 7 operation system that allows a user to automate simple tasks

Appleshare™

software that allows Apple Macintosh computers to share files and printers using a file server

AppleTalk™

proprietary communications protocol developed by Apple that carries data over network hardware between two or more Apple Macintosh computers and peripherals; similar to the seven-layer OSI protocol model; AppleTalk can link up to 32 devices and it uses a CSMA/CA design and transmits data at 230Kbps

AppleTalk Filing Protocol™ (AFP)

protocol used to communicate between workstations and servers in a network of Apple Macintosh computers

applet

(i) utility application program; (ii) (in Microsoft Windows) application started from the Control Panel

application

task which a computer performs or problem which a computer solves (as opposed to an operating system which is the way in which a computer works)

application developer
programmer who designs the look of an application and defines its functions

application file
binary file stored on disk that contains the machine code instructions of a program

application generator
special software that allows a programmer to define the main functions and look of an application; the generator then automatically creates the instructions to carry out the defined application

application icon
small image or graphical symbol that represents an application program in a graphical user interface

application icons

application orientated language
programming language that provides functions which allow the user to solve certain application problems

application package or program
set of computer programs and manuals that cover all aspects of a particular task (such as payroll, stock control, tax, etc.)

application programming interface (API)
set of standard program functions and commands that allow any programmer to interface a program with another application

application software *or* application program
program which is used by a user to make the computer do what is required; it is designed to allow a particular task to be performed

application specific integrated circuits (ASIC)
integrated circuit (chip) specially designed for one particular function or to special specifications

17

application terminal

terminal (such as at a sales desk) which is specially configured to carry out certain tasks

application window

application program running in a window displayed in a graphical user interface such as Microsoft's Windows

Arabic numbers *or* figures

figures such as 1, 2, 3, etc. (as opposed to the Roman numerals I, II, III, etc.)

arcade game

coin-operated console that runs a dedicated games software, with input device (normally a joystick), processor, graphics adapter and sound card built in

Archimedes™

personal computer developed by Acorn Computers; the Archimedes is based around a RISC central processor and is not compatible with either the IBM PC or Apple Macintosh

architecture

layout and interconnection of a computer's internal hardware and the logical relationships between CPU, memory and I/O devices

archived

(data) stored over a long period of time on backing storage (such as magnetic tape rather than a hard disk)

archive file

file containing data which is out of date, but which is kept for future reference

archive attribute *or* bit *or* flag

special attribute attached to a file in DOS and OS/2 that indicates if the file has been archived since it was last changed

area fill

(in graphics) instruction to fill an area of the screen or an enclosed shape with a colour or pattern

area graph

line graph drawn in which the area below the line is filled with a pattern or colour

arg
see
ARGUMENT

argument
variable acted upon by an operator or function; for example, if you enter the words 'MULTIPLY A, B', the processor will recognise the operator, MULTIPLY, and use it with the two arguments, A and B
see also
OPERAND

argument separator
punctuation mark or symbol that separates several arguments on one line

array
ordered structure containing individually accessible elements referenced by numbers, used to store tables or sets of related data

array processor
computer that can act upon several arrays of data simultaneously, for very fast mathematical applications

arrow keys
set of four keys on a keyboard that move the cursor or pointer around the screen; the four keys control movement up, down, left and right

arrow pointer
arrow-shaped cursor that is displayed to indicate the position on the screen

artifacts
very small errors in a digital version of an analog signal

artwork
graphical work or images

ASCII
AMERICAN STANDARD CODE FOR INFORMATION INTERCHANGE
code which represents alphanumeric characters with a standard set of codes
full listing of ASCII codes, see
APPENDIX

ASCII character
character which is in the ASCII list of codes

ASCII file

stored file containing only ASCII coded character data

ASCII text

letter and number characters with an ASCII code between 0 and 127

ASCIIZ string

a sequence of ASCII characters followed by the ASCII code zero that indicates the end of the sequence

ASIC

see
APPLICATION SPECIFIC INTEGRATED CIRCUIT

aspect ratio

ratio of the width to the height of a pixel or screen shapes; the aspect ratio of television is normally four units of width to every three units of height. This is expressed as 4 x 3 aspect ratio; a standard 35mm photographic negative frame measures 24 x 36 mm, which means it has three units of width to two units of height

assembly language

mnemonics which are used to represent machine code instructions (numbers that instruct the processor to carry out a particular operation)

assets

separate data elements (such as video, audio, image) that are used in a multimedia application

asymmetric system

(in video compression) a system that requires more equipment to compress the data than to decompress it.

Asymetrix™

software company that publishes the ToolBook authoring software package

AT

standard of PC originally developed by IBM that uses a 16-bit 80286 processor. AT originally meant IBM's Advanced Technology personal computer, but is now used to describe any IBM PC compatible that uses a 16-bit processor

AT-bus

expansion bus standard developed by IBM that uses an edge connector to carry 16-bits of data and address information

AT-keyboard
standard keyboard layout for IBM AT personal computers; the keyboard has 102 keys with a row of 12 function keys along the top

Atari ST™
range of personal computers developed by Atari Corporation; Atari ST computers use the 68000 range of processor and are not compatible with IBM PCs

ATM™
ADOBE TYPE MANAGER

attack
shape of the start of a sound signal with time
compare with
SUSTAIN, DECAY

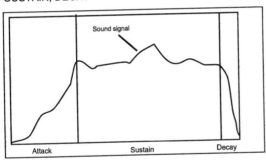

attack section of a sound signal

Attack   Sustain   Decay

attenuation
reduction or loss of signal strength; the difference between transmitted and received power measured in decibels

attribute
(i) (in printers, display) a single bit that defines whether the font has a particular characteristic, for example, whether it is displayed in normal, bold or underlined; (ii) (in a file) control bits of data stored with each file which control particular functions or aspects of the file such as whether it is a read-only, archived or system file

audible
which can be heard

audio

referring to sound or to things which can be heard; the human ear can hear a range of frequencies between around 20Hz-20KHz

audio board

See
SOUND CARD

audio cassette

reel of magnetic recording tape in a small protective casing inserted into a cassette recorder used for data storage in home computers or for analog audio signals

audio cassette recorder (ACR)

machine to transfer audio signals onto magnetic tape

audio file

digital sound sample stored on disk; often stored in WAV file format on a PC

audio response unit

speech synthesizer that allows a computer to speak responses to requests

audiotex

interactive voice response over the telephone in which a computer asks the caller questions and the caller responds by pressing numbers on his telephone

audio/video interleaved (AVI)

Windows multimedia video format developed by Microsoft; the system interleaves standard waveform audio and digital video frames (stored as bitmaps) to provide reduced speed animation at 15 frames per second at a resolution of 160x120 pixels in eight colours; audio is recorded at 11,025Hz, 8-bit samples.

audio/video interleaved (AVI) clip played back with the Media Player utility in Microsoft Windows

audiovisual (a/v)
audio and/or video capability

audio visual connection
see
AVC

author
person that creates a multimedia application using an authoring language or by writing a script

author level
mode of an authoring software package that is used by the author to design the application; the user uses the finished application at user level

authoring
creating a multimedia application by combining sound, video and images, usually using a script or authoring language

authoring language
programming language used to write multimedia applications or control a cast of multimedia objects and define how they react to a user's input

authoring system *or* software
set of tools normally used to develop multimedia applications; an authoring system provides special commands to control CD-ROM players, play sound files and video clips and display a user-friendly front-end

autoflow
(in DTP or wordprocessor) text that automatically flows around a graphic image or from one page to the next.

automatic gain
electronic circuit which automatically increases the volume when someone is speaking quietly and drops it when someone is speaking loudly

automatic volume control
see
AVC

autosizing
ability of a monitor to maintain the same rectangular image size when changing from one resolution to another

A/UX™

version of the Unix operating system for the Apple Macintosh range of computers

auxilliary audio device

audio device whose output is mixed with other waveforms, for example the output from a CD-audio

a/v

AUDIOVISUAL

AVC

AUDIO VISUAL CONNECTION

multimedia software developed by IBM that works with its Audio Capture and Video Capture boards

AVC

AUTOMATIC VOLUME CONTROL

electronic circuit that maintains constant sound level despite undesired differences in strength of incoming signal

AVI

AUDIO/VIDEO INTERLEAVED

Windows multimedia video format developed by Microsoft; the system interleaves standard waveform audio and digital video frames (stored as bitmaps) to provide reduced speed animation at 15 frames per second at a resolution of 160x120 pixels in eight colours; audio is recorded at 11,025Hz, 8-bit samples.

Bb

babble
crosstalk or noise from other sources which interferes with a signal

back projection
to project an image from behind a screen; often used in animation where the static scene is displayed with back projection, then the foreground characters are displayed and the composite scene photographed

backdrop
static background image in front of which are displayed actors or scenes

background
(i) base colour on screen or part of a picture which is behind the main object of interest; (ii) non-interactive processing in the computer; (iii) system in a computer where low-priority work can be done in the intervals when very important work is not being done

background image
image displayed as a backdrop behind a program or windows of a GUI; this image does not move and does not interfere with any programs or windows

background noise
noise which is present along with the required signal
see also
AMBIENT NOISE

background plane

see
BACKDROP

background reflectance

light reflected from a sheet of paper that is being scanned or read by an optical character reader

backlight

thin, flat light source placed behind a liquid crystal display (LCD) unit that improves the contrast of characters on the screen and allows it to be read in dim light

backlit display

a liquid crystal display (LCD) unit that has a backlight fitted to improve the contrast of the display

backup

to make a copy of important data onto a backing storage media in case the original is corrupted or damaged

backwards compatible

hardware device (normally a processor) that can still run all the same functions as earlier versions

band

range of frequencies between two limits

bandpass filter

electronic filter that allows a range of frequencies to pass, but attenuates all frequencies outside the specified range

bandwidth

(i) range of frequencies; (ii) measure of the amount of data that can be transmitted along a cable or channel or other medium; (iii) measure of the range of frequencies that a monitor or CRT will accept and display; high resolution monitors display more pixels per unit area which requires more data to be transmitted from the computer in the same period of time, and so a higher bandwidth

bar chart *or* bar graph

graph on which values are represented as vertical or horizontal bars

bar code *or* bar graphics
data represented as a series of printed stripes of varying widths

bar-code reader *or* optical scanner
optical device that reads data from a bar code

barrel
image distortion in which the image appears swollen in the middle and narrower at the top and the bottom

base 2
binary number system (using the two digits 0 and 1)

base 8
octal number system (using the eight digits 0 - 7)

base 10
decimal number system (using the ten digits 0 - 9)

base 16
hexadecimal number system (using the ten digits 0 - 9 and six letters A - F)

base font
default font and point size used by a word-processing program when no particular style or font has been selected

base hardware
minimum hardware requirements that a particular software package needs in order to run

base level synthesizer
(on a sound card) synthesizer that supports three melodic instruments and can play six notes simultaneously
compare with
EXTENDED LEVEL SYNTHESIZER

base memory *or* conventional memory *or* base RAM
(in an IBM-compatible PC) first 640Kb of random access memory in the PC
compare
HIGH MEMORY, EXPANDED MEMORY

baseband
(i) frequency range of a signal before it is processed or transmitted; (ii) digital

27

signals transmitted without modulation; (iii) information modulated with a single carrier frequency

baseline

(i) lines (that are only displayed during the design stage or author level of an application) which define the size and layout of a page in an application; (ii) horizontal line along which characters are printed or displayed; the descenders of a character drop below the line

BASIC

BEGINNER'S ALL-PURPOSE SYMBOLIC INSTRUCTION CODE
high-level programming language for developing programs in a conversational way, providing an easy introduction to computer programming
see also
VISUAL BASIC

basic input/output system

see
BIOS

BAT file extension

standard three-letter file extension used in MS-DOS systems to signify a batch file (a text file containing system commands)

bay *or* drive bay

space within a computer's casing where a disk drive, such as a CD-ROM drive, is fitted

beam

narrow light beam or electron rays; laser printers use a beam of laser light, CRTs use a beam of electrons to display an image

beam deflection

(in a CRT) movement of the electron beam across the inside of the screen

beep

audible warning noise

Beginner's All-Purpose Symbolic Instruction Code (BASIC)

high-level programming language for developing programs in a conversational way, providing an easy introduction to computer programming
see also
VISUAL BASIC

28

BEL
code for bell character (equivalent to ASCII code 7)

bell character
control code which causes a machine to produce an audible signal (equivalent to ASCII code 7, EBCDIC 2F).

benchmark
program used to test the performance of software or hardware or a system

Bernoulli™ drive *or* box
high capacity storage system using exchangeable cartridges

bespoke software
software that has been written especially for a customer's particular requirements

best fit
(i) (something) which is the nearest match to a requirement; (ii) function that selects the smallest free space in main memory for a requested virtual page

Beta™
first home VCR format developed by Sony; the system used 1/2-inch tape cassettes; the Beta standard is no longer produced and the prevalent home video standard is currently VHS

beta site
company or person that tests new software (before it is released) in a real environment to make sure it works correctly

beta software
version of software that has not finished all its testing before its release and so may still contain bugs

beta test
second stage of tests performed on a new software product just before it is due to be released
see also
ALPHA TEST

Bézier curve
geometric curve; the overall shape is defined by two midpoints, called control handles; Bézier curves are a feature of many high-end design software

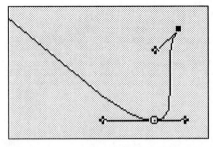

In a drawing program, Bézier curves are defined by moving bars to change the shape of the curve

packages; they allow a designer to create smooth curves by defining a number of points. The PostScript page description language uses Bézier curves to define the shapes of characters during printing.

bias
electrical reference level

binary digit
see
BIT

binary field
field (in a database record) that contains binary numbers; often refers to a field that is capable of holding any information, including data, text, graphics images, voice and video
see also
BLOB

binary large object
see
BLOB

binaural sound
method of recording sound so that it gives the impression of stereophony when played back

BIOS
BASIC INPUT/OUTPUT SYSTEM
software system-control routines that interface between high-level program instructions and the system peripherals to control the input and output to various standard devices, this often includes controlling the screen, keyboard and disk drives

bit

BINARY DIGIT

smallest unit in binary number notation, which can have the value 0 or 1

bitblt

BIT BLOCK TRANSFER

(in computer graphics) to move a block of bits from one memory location to another; if the computer has a memory-mapped display a bitblt effectively moves an image on screen

bit depth

number of bits used to represent the number of colours that can be displayed on a screen or printer at one time

bit depth	Total number of colours
4-bit	16
8-bit	256
16-bit	65,536
24-bit	16,777,216

bitmap

(i) image whose individual pixels can be controlled by changing the value of its stored bit (one is on, zero is off; in colour displays, more than one bit is used to provide control for the three colours - Red, Green, Blue); (ii) binary representation in which each bit or set of bits corresponds to some object

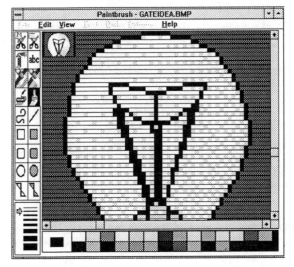

bitmap image displayed in a paint program

(image, font, etc.) or condition; (iii) file format for storing images in which data in the file represents the value of each pixel
compare with
VECTOR

bit-mapped font

font whose characters are made up of patterns of pixels
compare
VECTOR FONT

bitmp

see
BITMAP

bit plane

(in computer graphics) one layer of a multiple-layer image; each layer defines one colour of each pixel

bits per pixel (BPP)

number of bits assigned to store the colour of each pixel; one bit provides black or white, four bits gives 16 colour combinations, eight bits gives 256 colour combinations

black and white

(i) use of shades of grey to represent colours on a monitor or display; (ii) an image in which each pixel is either black or white with no shades of grey

black box

device that performs a function without the user knowing how

black matrix

CRT monitor tube in which the color phosphor dots are surrounded by black for increased contrast

blanking

period during which a screen displays nothing, in between two images or during the picture beam flyback

blit *or* bitblt

(in computer graphics) moving a block of bits from one memory location to another; if the computer has a memory-mapped display a bitblt effectively moves an image on screen

blitter

electronic component designed to process or move a bit-mapped image from one area of memory to another

blitting

transferring a bitmap image from a storage device to an output window

blob

BINARY LARGE OBJECT
field in a database record that can contain a large quantity of binary data - normally a bitmap image

BMP file

filename extension used to represent the Microsoft Windows standard for storing bitmap images

book

another name for a multimedia application

book mark

special character or code inserted at a particular point in a document that allows the user to move straight back to that point at a later date

book palette

set of colours that are are used in a particular multimedia application; two different applications could use different palettes and each must load its own palette otherwise the colours will appear corrupted

boolean

rules set down to define, simplify and manipulate logical functions based on statements which are true or false
see
AND, NOT, OR

boom

long metal arm that allows the operator to position a microphone close to the sound source; also used to position a video camera

boot up *or* booting

automatic execution of a set of instructions usually held in ROM when a computer is switched on; the boot instructions normally check the hardware and load the operating system software from disk

border

thin boundary line around a button or field or a graphic image

border style

attribute that determines the type of border around a button or field, for example single line, shadow or double-line are common border styles for a field

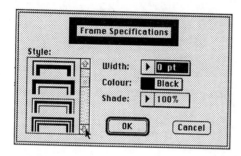

Range of border styles around a frame in a DTP layout

bounding box

rectangle that determines the size, position and shape of a graphic image or video clip

BPP

see
BITS PER PIXEL

branching

(in a program or script) decision with two or more possible results that lead to two different points in the program

break key

(in MCI) keystroke that interrupts a wait operation; by default, this is Ctrl-Break on a PC but can be modified using the MCI_BREAK command

breakpoint

(i) symbol inserted into a program which stops its execution at that point to allow registers, variables and memory locations to be examined (used when debugging a program); (ii) halt command inserted into a program to stop execution temporarily, allowing the programmer to examine data and registers while debugging a program; (iii) special character used to provide a breakpoint in a program (the debugging program allows breakpoint symbols to be inserted, it then executes the program until it reaches one, then halts)

34

broadband
(in local area networks or communications) transmission method that combines several channels of data onto a carrier signal and can carry the data over long distances

broadcast network
network for sending data to a number of receivers

broadcast quality
video image or signal that is the same as that used by professional television stations

browse mode
mode of operation in multimedia software that allows a user to move between pages in no fixed order

browser
software utility or front-end that allows a user to easily access and search through text or a database

browsing
moving through text or a multimedia application in no particular order, controlled by the user

brush
(in a paint program) most basic image-creation tool that draws a line of user-selectable colour and width on screen; most paint or graphics packages let you select a variety of sizes and shapes for the brush

buffer
area of memory used for temporary data storage

built-in message
message generated by a system or authoring language in response to an action (such as a mouse click)

bug
error in a computer program which makes it run incorrectly

bullet
symbol (often a filled circle or square) in front of a line of text, used to draw attention to a particular line in a list

bundle

package containing a computer together with software or accessories offered at a special price

bureau

(i) office which specializes in keyboarding data or processing batches of data for other small companies; (ii) company that specializes in typesetting from disks or outputting DTP or graphics files to bromide or film

bus

communication link consisting of a set of leads or wires which connect different parts of a computer hardware system, and over which data is transmitted and received by various circuits in the system

bus master

device that controls the bus whilst transmitting (bus master status can move between sending stations); normally this is the central processor, but in high-performance computers, secondary processors in a network card or graphics adapter can take over control of the bus from the CPU

see also

EISA, LOCAL BUS, MCA

button

normally, a square shape displayed on screen (or an area of the screen) that will carry out a particular action if selected by the user with a pointer or keyboard

see also

CHECKBOX, HOTSPOT, PUSH BUTTON, RADIO BUTTON

byte

group of bits or binary digits (usually eight) which a computer operates on as a single unit

Cc

C
high level programming language developed mainly for writing structured systems programs (the C language was originally developed for the UNIX operating system); Visual C is a Microsoft product that includes a code-generator to create C code for Windows-based applications

C++
high level programming language based on its predecessor, C, but providing object oriented programming functions

C-format
popular, broadcast-quality videotape format that uses 1-inch magnetic tape to store analog video recordings; often used before conversion to digital format

CAD
COMPUTER-AIDED DESIGN
software that allows a designer to accurately draw objects on screen

caddy
see
CD CADDY

CAI
COMPUTER-AIDED INSTRUCTION
software that helps teach a student a subject

CAL
COMPUTER-ASSISTED LEARNING
software that is used with normal teaching methods (books, exercises, classroom lectures) to help teach a student a subject

call
to transfer control to a separate program or routine from a main program

call handler
see
HANDLER

CAM
COMPUTER-ASSISTED MANUFACTURING
use of a computer to control machinery or assist in a manufacturing process

camcorder
compact, portable video camera with built-in video cassette recorder and microphone; records onto VHS, S-VHS or Hi-8 format cassettes and is normally for home use

caption
descriptive text that appears at the very top of a window or on a button or below an image

caption generator
computer or electronic device that allows a user to add titles or captions to a video sequence

capstan
spindle of a tape player or tape backup unit that keeps the tape pressed against the magnetic read/write head or pinch roller

capture
(i) action of obtaining data (either by keyboarding or by scanning or often automatically from a recording device or peripheral); (ii) to store the image currently displayed on screen in a file, useful when creating manuals about a software product; NOTE: in Windows, you can capture the current screen to the Clipboard by pressing the PrtScrn key; on a Macintosh you can capture the current screen by pressing Shift-Option-3

card
(i) board with electronic circuit that plugs into an expansion connector in a

computer and allows the computer to communicate with another device or expands the computer's functionality; (ii) single page within a HyperCard program; each card can have text, images, sound, video and buttons on it

carpal tunnel syndrome
see
RSI

carrier
continuous high frequency waveform that can be modulated by a signal

cartesian coordinates
positional system that uses two axes at right angles to represent a point which is located with two numbers, giving a position on each
compare with
POLAR COORDINATES

cascading menu
secondary menu that is displayed to the side of the main pull-down menu

cascading windows
(in a GUI) multiple windows that are displayed overlapping so that only the title bar at the top of each window is showing

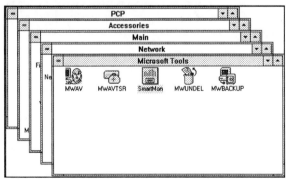

cascading windows

cast
collection of individual images, graphical objects and text that are used in a multimedia presentation

cast-based animation
type of animation in which everything is an object and has its defined movement, colour, shape, etc; a script controls the actions of each object

cast member
a single object within a cast used in a presentation, such as text, an image or an animated object

cathode ray tube
see
CRT

CAV
see
CONSTANT ANGULAR VELOCITY

CBL
COMPUTER-BASED LEARNING
education or learning using special programs running on a computer

CBT
COMPUTER-BASED TRAINING
use of a computer system to train students

CCD
CHARGE-COUPLED DEVICE
electronic device that has an array of tiny elements whose electrical charge changes with light; each element represents a pixel and its state can be examined to record the light intensity at that point; used in video cameras

CCIR 601
recommended standard for defining digital video

CD
COMPACT DISC
see
CD-ROM

CD
CHDIR *OR* CHANGE DIRECTORY
system instruction in MS-DOS and UNIX that moves you around a directory structure; for example, CD.. moves up one directory

CD-audio
see
CD DA

CD-bridge

extension to the CD-ROM XA standard that allows extra data to be added so that the disc can be read on a CD-i player

CD caddy

flat plastic container that holds a CD-ROM disc; the container is inserted into the CD-ROM disc drive; NOTE: some CD-ROM drives use a CD caddy to hold the disc, others use a motorised tray on which you place the disc

CD DA

COMPACT DISC DIGITAL AUDIO

(also called Red Book audio) standard that provides 73 minutes of high quality digital sound on a CD at a sample rate of 44.1KHz

CD+Graphics *or* CD+G

CD format that adds a text track to an audio disc - used to store song title information

CD-i

COMPACT DISC INTERACTIVE

CD-ROM system developed by Philips aimed for home use; the disc provides similar features to the CD-ROM XA standard; the system includes a central unit with a drive, processor, display hardware and electronics to connect to a television; CD-i is a mix of hardware and software standards that combine sound, data, video and text onto a CD-ROM and allow a user to interact with the software stored on a CD-ROM; the standard defines encoding, compression and display functions

CD-i digital audio

a CD-i disc can record audio in digital format in one of four ways: mono or stereo and at two different sample rates

CD-i digital images

the compression method used to store images and video frames on a CD-i disc

CD-i disc

CD-ROM that contains video, text, images and sound and is read with a CD-i player

CD-i player

console that contains all the drive, processing and display electronics to read a CD-i disc and display images on a normal television; users interact either through a track-ball, joystick or mouse

CD-i sector
unit of storage on a CD-i disc that can store 2352 bytes

CD-R
RECORDABLE COMPACT DISC
technology that allows a user to write data to and read from a CD-R disc; a CD-R disc can be played in any standard CD-ROM drive but needs a special CD-R drive to write data to the disc; a high-powered laser is normally used to burn holes into the surface to represent the digital data

CD real time operating system
see
CDRTOS

CD-ROM *or* CD
COMPACT DISC READ ONLY MEMORY
small plastic disc that is used as a high capacity ROM storage device that can store 650Mb of data; data is stored in binary form as holes etched on the surface which are then read by a laser; CD-ROM drives normally have an access time of between 150-300 milliseconds, compared to under 15ms for a fast hard disk drive; a single-speed disc spins at 230rpm
See also
CD-ROM XA, CD-I, DVI

CD-ROM drive
disc drive that allows a computer to read data stored on a CD-ROM; the player spins the disc and uses a laser beam to read etched patterns on the surface of the CD-ROM that represent data bits

CD-ROM Extended Architecture *or* CD-ROM XA
enhanced CD-ROM format developed by Philips, Sony and Microsoft, that allows data to be read from the disc at the same time as audio is played back; the standard defines how audio, images and data are stored on a CD-ROM disc to allow sound and video to be accessed at the same time; CD-ROM XA drives can read a Kodak Photo CD disc. CD-ROM XA discs can be played on a CD-i player; a CD-ROM XA disc can be read in a standard CD-ROM player, but requires a special CD-ROM XA controller card

CD-ROM Extensions
software required to allow an operating system (typically DOS) to access a CD-ROM drive attached to a PC

CD-ROM mode 1
standard, original method of storing data in the High Sierra file format

CD-ROM mode 2
higher capacity storage format that stores data in the space used in mode 1 for error correction; neither mode 1 nor mode 2 can play audio and simultaneously read data - hence the XA extension

CD-ROM player
disc drive that allows a computer to read data stored on a CD-ROM; the player uses a laser beam to read etched patterns on the surface of the CD-ROM that represent data bits

CD-ROM XA *or* CD-XA
CD-ROM EXTENDED ARCHITECTURE
enhanced CD-ROM format developed by Philips, Sony and Microsoft, that allows data to be read from the disc at the same time as audio is played back; the standard defines how audio, images and data are stored on a CD-ROM disc to allow sound and video to be accessed at the same time; CD-ROM XA drives can read a Kodak Photo CD disc. CD-ROM XA discs can be played on a CD-i player; a CD-ROM XA disc can be read in a standard CD-ROM player, but requires a special CD-ROM XA controller card

CDRTOS
CD REAL TIME OPERATING SYSTEM
operating system used to run a CD-i hardware platform

CD-V
COMPACT DISC VIDEO
format for storing 5 minutes of video data on a 3-inch disc in analog form (this format is no longer used)

CD-WO
COMPACT DISC WRITE ONCE
CD-ROM disc and drive technology that allows a user to write data to the disc once only and is useful for storing archived documents or for testing a CD-ROM before it is duplicated

CDTV
COMMODORE DYNAMIC TOTAL VISION
CD-ROM standard developed by Commodore that combines audio, graphics and text; this standard is mainly intended as an interactive system for home use; the player connects to a television and can also play music CDs

CD32
unit with a processor and CD-ROM drive developed by Commodore that uses its Amiga computer - aimed at the games market

cel
single frame within an animation sequence

central processing unit
see
CPU

CGA
COLOUR GRAPHICS ADAPTER
video display standard developed by IBM that provided low-resolution text and graphics; now superseded by EGA and VGA; the CGA standard could diplay images at a resolution of 320x200 pixels
see also
APPENDIX

CGM
COMPUTER GRAPHICS METAFILE
device-independent file format that provides one method of storing an image as a collection of separate objects

channel
(i) (in a graphics application) term used to refer to an individual plane within an image that can store a matte or special effect or one part of the final picture; (ii) (in MIDI) method of identifying individual tracks or instruments in a MIDI setup; there are 16 channel numbers and an instrument can be set to respond to the instructions on one particular channel; each channel also has a patch associated with it that defines the sound that is played; (iii) (in animation or video editing software) method of organising cast members in a presentation; each channel can hold a cast member, background or a special effect according to time - these are played back together to create the final presentation

channel map
(in Windows MIDI Mapper utility) list that shows which MIDI channel is being redirected to another

character generator
ROM that provides the display circuits with a pattern of dots which represent the character (block)

characters per inch

see
CPI

charge-coupled device

see
CCD

checkbox

(in a GUI or front-end) small box displayed with a cross inside it if the option
has been selected, or empty if the option is not selected; unlike a radio button,
more than one checkbox can be selected
see also
BUTTON

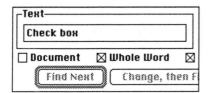

*Checkbox displays a cross in a box if a
user selects the option*

check mark

indicator in a checkbox that shows if the checkbox has been selected; often a
cross or tick

child process

second program run from within another program; for example, in some DOS
applications you can return to the DOS prompt, whilst the main program is still
running: the DOS prompt is a child process that has been started by running a
second copy of the DOS command interpreter

child window

window within a main window; the smaller window cannot be moved outside
the boundary of the main window and is closed when the main window is
closed

chip

electronic device consisting of a small piece of a crystal of a semiconductor
onto which are etched or manufactured (by doping) a number of components
such as transistors, resistors and capacitors, which together perform a
function

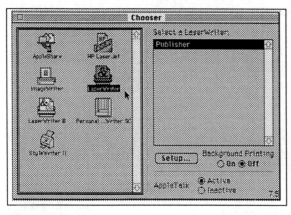

The Chooser utility in a Macintosh allows a user to select a printer or network server

Chooser™
operating system utility supplied with the Apple Macintosh that allows a user to select the active printer, network and peripheral from a selection that are connected

chord keying
action of pressing two or more keys at the same time to perform a function

chroma
measure of the hue and saturation of a colour

chroma key *or* colour key
(in video) special effect in which an object is photographed against a (normally blue) background which is then replaced with another image to give the impression that the object appears against the image; for example, to give the appearance of flying, you could record a video sequence of a person against a blue background, then electronically replace this blue background colour (the chroma key) with footage of sky

chromatic
referring to colours

chrominance
hue and saturation of an image; often represented as signals, U (hue), V (saturation) and Y (luminance)

chrominance signal
part of a colour video signal containing the hue and saturation data of a colour

chunk

basic part of a RIFF file that consists of an indentifier (chunk ID) and data

CIF

videophone ISDN standard which displays colour images at a resolution of 352x288 pixels; this standard uses two ISDN B channels

cine film

normally refers to 8mm or 16mm photographic film used to record motion pictures with an optional sound track

cine-oriented

(in a film or video clip) orientation of the image that is parallel to the outside edge of the medium

CIS

CONTACT IMAGE SENSOR

scanner in which the detectors (a flat bar of light-sensitive diodes) touch the original, without any lens that might distort the image

CISC

COMPLEX INSTRUCTION SET COMPUTER

central processor chip that can carry out a large number of instructions each of which does a complete job; this compares with a RISC processor which has fewer simple instructions that are executed more quickly but is often more complex to program

clamper

circuit which limits the level of a signal from a scanning head or other input device to a maximum before this is converted to a digital value; used to cut out noise and spikes

class

(in a programming language) definition of what a particular software routine will do or what sort of variable it can operate on

click

(i) pressing a key or button on a keyboard or mouse; (ii) to select a button or menu option on screen by moving the pointer over the object and pressing the mouse button
see also
DOUBLE-CLICK

client application
application that can accept linked or embedded objects from a server application
see
OLE

client area
(in a GUI) area inside a window that can be used to display graphics or text

client-server architecture
distribution of processing power in which a central server computer carries out the main tasks in response to instructions from terminals or workstations; the results are sent back across the network to be displayed on the terminal, the client (the terminal or workstation) does not need to be able to access directly the data stored on the server nor does it need to carry out a lot of processing

clip-art
set of pre-drawn images or drawings that a user can incorporate into a presentation

clipboard
(i) temporary storage area for data; (ii) (in Microsoft Windows and Macintosh Finder) utility that temporarily stores any type of data, such as a word or an image

clipping
cutting off the outer edges of an image or the highest and lowest parts of a signal

clock cycle
time period between two consecutive clock pulses

clock doubler
component that doubles the speed of the main system clock to effectively double the processing speed of the computer

clock pulse
regular pulse used for timing or synchronizing purposes

clock rate *or* speed
number of pulses that a clock generates every second

clock track

line of recorded marks on a disk or tape which provides data about the read head location

clocked signals

signals that are synchronized with a clock pulse

CLS

(in MS-DOS) system command to clear the screen, leaving the system prompt and cursor at the top left-hand corner of the screen

cluster

one or more sectors on a hard disk that are used to store a file or part of a file

CLUT

COLOUR LOOK-UP TABLE

table of values that define the colours in a palette; this allows a program to use colours without having to calculate them each time

CLV

see
CONSTANT LINEAR VELOCITY

CMYK

CYAN-MAGENTA-YELLOW-BLACK

(in graphics or DTP) method of describing a colour by the percentage content of its four component colours
see also
YMCK, RGB, HSV

co-axial cable *or* coax

cable made up of a central core, surrounded by an insulating layer then a second shielding conductor; co-axial cable is used for high frequency, low loss applications including television transmission, audio connections and network cabling; co-ax cable provides a higher bandwidth than twisted-pair cabling

codec

(CODER-DECODER)

electronic device that converts an audio or video signal into a digital form (and vice versa) using various analogue to digital conversion techniques such as pulse code modulation
see also
A/D, D/A, PCM

49

collaboration

two or more people working together to produce or use a multimedia application

colour

sensation sensed by the eye, due to its response to various frequencies of light; NOTE: the stroke colour is the colour displayed when a line is drawn in a graphics program or a brush tool is used; fill colour is the colour used when filling an area of an image with colour; true colour normally refers to 24-bit colour image

colour bits

number of data bits assigned to a pixel to describe its colour; one bit provides two colours, two bits provide four colours and eight bits allow 256 colour combinations

colour cell

smallest area on a CRT screen that can display colour information

colour cycling

to change the colours in a palette over a period of time, normally used to create a special effect or animation

colour graphics adapter

see
CGA
>APPENDIX: PC GRAPHICS

colour printer

printer that can produce hard copy in colour; includes colour ink-jet, colour dot-matrix and thermal-transfer printers

colour saturation

purity of a colour signal

colour key

image manipulation technique used to superimpose one image on another; often used with two video sources to create special effects - one image is photographed against a blue (matte) background which is then superimposed with another image to produce a combined picture
see also
CHROMA KEY, MATTE

colour depth

number of bits used to describe the colour of a pixel; for example, if four bits are used to describe each pixel, it can support 16 different colours and has a depth of 4-bits

colour look-up table (CLUT)

table of values that define the colours in a palette, this allows a program to use colours without having to calculate them each time

colour palette

range of colours which can be used (on a printer or display)

colour separation

separating a colour image into its constituent colours in order to produce printing plates for colour printing; full colour printing needs four-colour separation to produce four printing plates for the cyan, magenta, yellow and black (CMYK) inks that together create a colour image

colour standard

one of three international standards used to describe how colour TV and video images are displayed and transmitted: NTSC, PAL and SECAM

colour tool

utility or icon in a graphics or DTP application that allows the user to create custom colours by specifying the CMYK or RGB values and then draw or fill an area with this colour

column report

viewing data in columns; each column is one field of a record and each row a separate record

COM

COMPUTER OUTPUT MICROFILM
to record data from a computer onto microfilm or microfiche

combi player

hardware drive that can read two or more different CD-ROM formats

combo box

box that displays a number of different input and output objects; for example, a list of options, together with radio buttons and a field in which the user can type their request

comic-strip oriented

film-image orientation in which the image runs perpendicular to the outer edge
of the film
compare with
CINE-ORIENTED

command

word or action entered to carry out an operation

command driven

(software) that is controlled by the user typing in command words rather than
making a selection from a menu

command line interface

user interface in which the user controls the operating system (or program) by
typing in commands; for example, DOS is a command line interface, Windows
is a graphical user interface that can be controlled by using a mouse
compare with
GUI

command message

(in MCI) character or symbol that represents an MCI command

command string

(in MCI) character string that contains all the information to carry out an MCI
command; the string ends with a null character and is split by MCI into the
command message and data structure

command window

window that allows a user to enter commands to control the low-level
operation of a program, normally whilst another window displays the result

command window history

list of previous commands entered in the command window

comment

(in a program or script) line added to explain a feature to a programmer; the
line is not executed

Commodore Dynamic Total Vision (CDTV)

CD-ROM standard developed by Commodore that combines audio, graphics
and text; this standard is mainly intended as an interactive system for home
use; the player connects to a television and can also play music CDs

common intermediate format (CIF)
videophone ISDN standard which displays colour images at a resolution of 352x288 pixels; this standard uses two ISDN B channels

compact disc
see
CD-ROM

compact disc video
see
CD-V

compact disc write once
see
CD-WO

compiler
software that translates a high-level language into machine code that will run directly on a processor

complex instruction set computer
see
CISC

composite video
video part of a television signal (that does not contain any audio signal) produced by mixing the red, green, blue and a synchronising clock signal together; a composite video display is not as clear or crisp as a display that uses separate red, green and blue signals from a computer or a video source

compound device
Windows MCI multimedia device that requires a data file, such as a sound card that plays back a WAV file controlled by the waveform audio driver

compound document
document that contains information created by several other applications; for example, if you write a letter using a wordprocessor then embed a WAV file voice message the result is a compound document; the technology to support compound documents was developed with Microsoft Windows 3.1 which included OLE, a feature that allows data from one application to be embedded in a document
see also
OLE

53

compound file

individual files grouped together in one file

compressed video

video signals that have been compressed to reduce the data rate required to transmit the information; a normal television picture is transmitted at around 50-90Mbits/second, a compressed video signal can be transmitted at around one tenth of the data rate

compression

to reduce the size of a data file (often a graphics image) by encoding the data in a more efficient way
see also
RLE

compression ratio

ratio of the size of an original, uncompressed file to the final, compressed file that has been more efficiently encoded

computer-aided design

see
CAD

computer-aided instruction

see
CAI

computer-assisted learning

see
CAL

computer-assisted manufacturing

see
CAM

computer-based learning

see
CBL

computer-based training

see
CBT

computer graphics metafile
see
CGM

computer system
hardware elements and peripherals that make up a computer and its associated parts; for example, a processor unit, disk drive, printer, keyboard and monitor

concatenate
to join together two files or variables

concatenation operator
instruction that joins two pieces of data or variables together

concurrency
data or resources that are accessed by more than one user or application at the same time

console
normally refers to the electronic hardware of a video game contained in a compact box, with a processor, drive, graphics and sound generator electronics

constant
item of data, whose value does not change (as opposed to a variable)

constant angular velocity (CAV)
CD-ROM that spins at a constant speed; the size of each data frame on the disc varies so as to maintain a regular data throughput of one frame per second; any frame will be slightly larger than the one after it and slightly smaller than the one before it
compare with
CONSTANT LINEAR VELOCITY

constant linear velocity (CLV)
disk technology in which the disk spins at different speeds according to the track that is being accessed; by varying the speed of the disk, the physical density of bits in each track remains the same, so the tracks at the outer edge of the disk hold more data than the inner tracks; CLV is normally used with CD-ROM drives
compare with
CONSTANT ANGULAR VELOCITY

constrain
limits set that define the maximum movement of an object on screen

consumables
small cheap extra items required in the day-to-day running of a computer system (such as paper and printer ribbons)

consumer market
potential market for a product that is based on the general public buying advertised products from a shop rather than a specialist or academic market

contact image sensor (CIS)
scanner in which the detectors (a flat bar of light-sensitive diodes) touch the original, without any lens that might distort the image

container
something that can be set to a value; for example, a variable is a container, as is an object's colour or position or other properties

content
text, images, sound, video and information within a database or multimedia application

content provider
company or person who owns the copyright of text or images in an application

context-sensitive help
help message that gives useful information about the particular function or part of the program you are in rather than general information about the whole program

context-switching
process in which several programs are loaded in memory, but only one at a time can be executed: COMMENT: unlike a true multitasking system which can load several programs into memory and run several programs at once, context-switching only allows one program to be run at a time

contiguous graphics
graphic cells or characters which touch each other

contouring
(i) (in a graphics application) process that converts a wire-frame drawing into a solid-looking object by adding shadows and texture; (ii) (in a graphics

application) function that creates realistic-looking ground or a surface, for example to create the ground in a virtual-reality system

contrast
(i) difference between black and white tones or between colours; (ii) control knob on a display that alters the difference between black and white tones or between colours

contrast enhancement filter
special filter put over a monitor to increase contrast and prevent eye-strain

control change
(in MIDI) message sent to a synthesizer to instruct it to change a setting, for example to change the volume of a MIDI channel

control character
special character that provides a control sequence rather than an alphanumeric character; normally a non-printing character that changes the appearance of text

control key *or* Ctrl
(on IBM-PC compatible systems) special key (in the lower left corner) that provides a secondary function when pressed with another key
see also
CTRL-ALT-DEL

control menu
(in Microsoft Windows) menu that allows you to move, resize or close the current window; the menu is accessed by pressing Alt-Space

control panel
(i) main computer system control switches and status indicators; (ii) (in Windows, Macintosh and OS/2) utility that displays the user-definable options such as keyboard, country-code and type of mouse

control structure
set of instructions that are run in a particular circumstance; an IF..THEN statement selects a particular control structure depending on the value of a variable

conventional memory *or* RAM
(in an IBM-PC compatible system) the random access memory region installed in a PC from 0 up to 640Kb; this area of memory can be directly controlled by

MS-DOS and it is where most programs are loaded when they are executed
compare
HIGH MEMORY, EXPANDED MEMORY

convergence

a measure of how accurately the three colour beams (red, green, blue) in a colour monitor align and track when drawing an image on the screen
see also
FOCUS, DOT PITCH

conversion tables

see
TRANSLATION TABLES

coprocessor

extra, specialized processor, such as a numerical processor that can work with a main CPU to increase execution speed

copyright

legal right (lasting for fifty years after the death of an artist whose work has been published) which a writer or programmer has in his own work, allowing him not to have it copied without the payment of royalties (now extended to 70 years in the EU)

Copyright Act

(in the UK) Act of Parliament making copyright legal, and controlling the copying of copyright material

corona

electric discharge that is used to charge the toner within a laser printer

corona wire

thin wire that charges the powdered toner particles in a laser printer as they pass across it

corporate video

video produced for internal training or as a publicity tool for a company and not intended to be broadcast

country file

file within an operating system that defines the parameters (such as character set and keyboard layout) for different countries

```
Courier
Sample text formatted in the Courier font.
This represents a mono-spaced font that is
similar to that of a typewriter.
—
```
*Courier
font*

Courier
fixed-space or monospace typeface that is similar to the type produced by an office typewriter

courseware
software, manuals and video that make up a training package or CAL product

cpi
CHARACTERS PER INCH
number of printed characters which fit within a space one inch wide

CPU
CENTRAL PROCESSING UNIT
group of circuits which perform the basic functions of a computer, made up of three parts: the control unit, the arithmetic and logic unit and the input/output unit; in a file handling program CPU time might be minimal, since data retrieval (from disk) would account for a large part of the program run; in a mathematical program, the CPU time could be much higher in proportion to the total run time. Multimedia programs tend to require fast hard disk and video systems rather than a fast CPU (unless complex graphics are calculated).

CPU cycle
period of time taken to fetch and execute an instruction (usually a simple ADD instruction) used as a measure of computer speed

crop
to reduce the size or margins of an image or to cut out a rectangular section of an image

crop marks
(in DTP software) printed marks that show the edge of a page or image and allow it to be cut accurately

crosshair
cursor in the shape of a cross, used to indicate the position on screen normally

displayed when drawing in a CAD program

CRT

CATHODE RAY TUBE

device used for displaying characters or figures or graphical information, similar to a TV set; cathode ray tubes are used in television sets, computer monitors and VDUs; a CRT consists of a vacuum tube, one end of which is flat and coated with phosphor, the other end containing an electron beam source. Characters or graphics are visible when the controllable electron beam strikes the phosphor causing it to glow

crystal

small slice of quartz crystal which vibrates at a certain frequency, used as a very accurate clock signal for computer or other high precision timing applications

crystal shutter printer

page printer that uses a powerful light controlled by a liquid crystal display to produce an image on a photo-sensitive drum
see also
LASER PRINTER

CTRL *or* Ctrl key

CONTROL KEY

(on IBM-PC compatible systems) special key (in the lower left corner) that provides a secondary function when pressed with another key

Ctrl-Alt-Del

pressing these three keys at once will cause a PC to carry out a soft reset

cue

prompt or message displayed on a screen to remind the user that an input is expected

cursor

marker on a display device which shows where the next character will appear; cursors can take several forms, such as a square of bright light, a bright underline or a flashing light
see also
CROSSHAIR, I-BEAM, POINTER

cursor control keys

keys on a keyboard that allow the cursor to be moved in different directions

cursor home

movement of the cursor to the top left hand corner of the screen

cursor pad

group of cursor control keys

cursor resource

image that is displayed as a cursor; programming languages and authoring tools normally provide a range of different cursor images that a developer can use: for example, an egg-timer cursor when waiting or an arrow when pointing

custom colours

range of colours in a palette that are used by an image or application
see also
SYSTEM PALETTE

cut

(in video) to switch from one scene to another in two consequtive frames, with no special transition effect (such as a fade)

cut-and-paste

selecting section of text or data, copying it to the clipboard, then moving to another point or document and inserting it (often used in word-processors and DTP packages for easy page editing)

cyan-magenta-yellow-black

see
CMYK

Dd

D1 videotape
19mm videotape format used for professional, digital recordings

DAC *or* D/A converter
DIGITAL TO ANALOG CONVERTER
circuit that converts a digital signal to an analog one (the analog signal is proportional to the input binary number)

daisy-chain
method of connecting equipment with a cable passing from one to the next rather than separate cables; this is the method used to connect SCSI devices and Ethernet networks

daisy-wheel printer
printer which uses a disc with spokes, each spoke has a character shape at its end; the printer spins the disc to the correct spoke, then strikes the charcter against an inked riboon onto the paper

DAT
DIGITAL AUDIO TAPE
compact cassette, smaller than an audio cassette, that provides a system of recording sound as digital information onto magnetic tape with very high-quality reproduction; also used as a high-capacity tape backup system that can store 1.3Gb of data; sound is recorded at a sample rate of either 32, 44.1 or 48KHz to provide up to two hours of CD-quality sound

DAT drive
drive that records data onto a DAT tape in digital form

data
collection of facts made up of numbers, characters and symbols, stored on a computer in such a way that it can be processed by the computer. Data is different from information in that it is formed of facts stored in machine-readable form. When the facts are processed by the computer into a form which can be understood by people, the data becomes information

data acquisition
converting original image, sound or text into a digital form

data buffer
temporary storage location for data received by a device that is not yet ready to accept it

data bus
electrical bus carrying the data between a CPU and memory and peripheral devices

data capture
act of obtaining data (either by keyboarding or by scanning, or often automatically from a recording device or peripheral)

data compacting
reducing the space taken by data by coding it in a more efficient way

data compression
means of reducing size of data by removing spaces, empty sections and unused material from the blocks of data

data delimiter
special symbol or character that marks the end of a file or data item

data description language (DDL)
part of database system software which describes the structure of the system and data

data dictionary/directory (DD/D)
software which gives a list of types and forms of data contained within a database

data input bus
see
DIB

data integrity
ensuring data is correct, not damaged and not corrupt

data item
one unit of data such as the quantity of items in stock, a person's name, age or occupation

data glove
electronic glove that fits over a user's hand and contains sensors that transmit the position of the user's hand and fingers to a computer, most often used in a virtual reality system

data projector
device that uses three large coloured lights (red, green and blue) to project a colour image output from a computer onto a large screen; compare this with a flat-panel display, a colour LCD screen which is placed on an overhead projecter to display an image on a larger screen

Data Protection Act
legislation passed in 1984 in the UK demanding that owners of a database that contains personal details must register with a central Government agency

data transfer rate
rate at which data is moved from one point to another

data type
the sort of data which can be stored in a register (such as string, number, etc.)

database
integrated collection of files of data stored in a structured form in a large memory, which can be accessed by one or more users at different terminals

database administrator (DBA)
person in charge of running and maintaining a database system

database engine
program that provides an interface between a program written to access the functions of a DBMS and the DBMS

database management system

see
DBMS

DBA

see
DATABASE ADMINISTRATOR

dBASE™

popular database software that includes a built-in programming language; dBASE has several versions, II, III and IV; the software development is currently carried out by Borland International, files created in dBASE can normally be imported into other database programs

DBMS

DATABASE MANAGEMENT SYSTEM
series of software utilities that allow a user to create, organise and search for data in a database

DCC

DIGITAL COMPACT CASSETTE
magnetic tape in a compact cassette box that is used to store computer data or audio signals in a digital format (DCC is the newer version of the traditional audio cassette, but it can record CD quality sound with its digital storage capability)

DD/D

see
DATA DICTIONARY/DIRECTORY

DDE

see
DIRECT DATA ENTRY

DDE

see
DYNAMIC DATA EXCHANGE

DDL

DATA DESCRIPTION LANGUAGE
part of database system software which describes the structure of the system and data

debugger
software that helps a programmer find faults or errors in a program

decay
the shape of a (sound) signal as it fades away

decibel *or* dB
unit for measuring the power of a sound or the strength of a signal (the decibel scale is logarithmic)

decompression
expanding a compressed image or data file so that it can be viewed

default
(i) predefined course of action or value that is assumed unless the operator alters it; (ii) value that is used by a program if the user does not make any changes to the settings; for example, an application may ask the user if he wants to install the application to the default, i.e. the C:\APP directory - the user can accept or change this

default drive
disk drive that is accessed first in a multi-disk system (to try and load the operating system or a program)

default option
preset value or option that is to be used if no other value has been specified

default palette *or* system colours
range of colours that are available on a particular system; a user or application can often change these to create their own palette range of colours

definition
ability of a screen to display fine detail
see also
RESOLUTION

defragmentation
reorganisation of files scattered across non-contiguous sectors on a hard disk; when a file is saved to disk, it is not always saved in adjacent sectors; this will increase the retrieval time. Defragmentation moves files back into adjacent sectors so that the read head does not have to move far across the disk, and it increases performance

defragmentation utility
software utility that carries out the process of defragmentation on a computer's hard disk

degauss
to remove unwanted magnetic fields and effects from magnetic tape, disks or read/write heads

degausser
device used to remove unwanted magnetic fields from a disk or tape or recording head

degradation
(i) loss of picture or signal quality; (ii) loss of picture contrast and quality due to signal distortion or bad copying of a video signal

dejagging
see
ANTI-ALIASING, JAGGIES

delete
to remove text or data or a file from a storage device

delimited-field file
data file in which each field is separated by a special character (often a tab character or comma) and each record is separated by a carriage return or a second special character; this allows data files to be transferred between database applications
see also
COMMA-DELIMITED

delimiter
(i) character or symbol used to indicate to a language or program the start or end of data or a record or information; (ii) the boundary between an instruction and its argument

delivery system
hardware and software required to play a particular multimedia title

delta YUV
digital video encoding technique in which luminance of a pixel is calculated by the RGB input signal (Y0.6G + 0.3R + 0.1B); from the value of Y, U and V are calculated as UR - Y; VB - Y

demo

DEMONSTRATION

showing how a piece of computer equipment or software works to a potential customer

demonstration software

software that shows what an application is like to use and what it can do, without implementing all the functions; typically this is with a limited set of data or it does not allow the user to save their work or only works for a short period of time

density

(i) darkness of an image; (ii) number of bits of data that can be stored per unit area on a disk

descrambler

device which produces a clear video signal from an encoded signal that is transmitted to prevent unauthorized viewing; normally used to receive television channels via a satellite dish - the viewer pays for the descrambler and can then watch certain television channels

desktop PC

normally refers to an IBM-compatible computer which can be placed on a user's desk: comprises a system unit (with main electronics, disk drive and controllers) and a separate monitor and keyboard. This contrasts with a laptop computer.

desktop media

combination of presentation graphics, desktop publishing and multimedia; this is a phrase that was originally used by Apple

desktop presentations

presentation graphics, text and charts produced and designed on a desktop personal computer
see also
PRESENTATION SOFTWARE

desktop publishing (DTP)

the design, layout and printing of documents, books and magazines using special software, a desktop computer and a high-resolution printer; the software normally provides a WYSIWYG preview to show what the printed page will look like

desktop video

software and hardware combination that allow a user to edit video; normally consits of a PC or Macintosh with a digitiser, editing software and control of external VCRs

Desktop video editing application with video players, transition effects and audio.

destination object

(in a drag and drop operation) the object or icon onto which you drop an object; many GUIs have a trashcan icon - a destination object onto which you drag and drop files that you want to delete

destination page

the target page within a hyperlink; when a user clicks on the active object in a hyperlink, the software displays the destination page

destructive readout

see
DRO

Deutsche Industrienorm
see
DIN

device dependent
software application that will not run correctly without a particular piece of hardware (for example, this could be video editing software that will not run if the PC is not connected to a video player, or a paint-package that needs a 24-bit graphics adapter)

device driver
program or routine used to interface and manage an I/O device or peripheral

device element
data required for an MCI compound device (normally a data file), for example a WAVE file that is played back through a sound card

device independent bitmap (DIB)
file format for a Windows graphics image that consists of a header, colour table (palette) and bitmap data; can be in 1, 4, 8 or 24-bit colour resolution

DGIS
DIRECT GRAPHICS INTERFACE STANDARD
standard graphics interface for video adapters, primarily used with the 340x0 range of graphics chips

DIA/DCA
DOCUMENT INTERCHANGE ARCHITECTURE/DOCUMENT CONTENT ARCHITECTURE
standard method for the transmission and storage of documents, text and video over networks; part of the IBM SNA range of standards

diagnostic message
message that appears to explain the type, location and probable cause of a software error or hardware failure

diaphragm
thin flexible sheet which vibrates in response to sound waves to create an electrical signal (as in a microphone) or in response to electrical signals to create sound waves (as in a speaker)

dialect
slight variation of a standard language; programming languages from different

manufacturers often contain slight differences and enhancements when compared to the standard

dialogue *or* dialog
speech or speaking to another person; communication between devices such as computers

dialog box
on-screen message from a program to the user

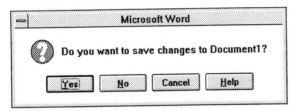

dialog box

DIB
DEVICE INDEPENDENT BITMAP
file format for a Microsoft Windows graphics image that consists of a header, colour table (palette) and bitmap data; can be in 1, 4, 8 or 24-bit colour

DIB
DATA INPUT BUS
bus used when transferring data from one section of a computer to another, such as between memory and CPU

dibit
digit made up of two binary bits

dichotomizing search
fast search method that is used on ordered list of data (the method works as follows: the search key is compared with the data in the middle of the list and one half is discarded, this is repeated with the half remaining until only one data item remains)

dictionary
(i) book which lists words and their meanings; (ii) data management structure which allows files to be referenced and sorted; (iii) part of a spelling checker program: list of correctly spelled words against which the text is checked
see also
SPELL-CHECKER

DIF file

DATA INTERCHANGE FORMAT

de facto standard that defines the way a spreadsheet, its formula and data are stored in a file

differential pulse coded modulation (DPCM)

method of encoding an analogue signal into a digital form in which the value recorded is equal to the difference between the current sample and the previous sample

digital

which represents data or physical quantities in numerical form (especially using a binary system in computer related devices)

digital audio tape (DAT)

compact cassette, smaller than an audio cassette, that provides a system of recording sound as digital information onto magnetic tape with very high-quality reproduction; also used as a high-capacity tape backup system that can store 1.3Gb of data; sound is recorded at a sample rate of either 32, 44.1 or 48KHz to provide up to two hours of CD-quality sound

digital camera

(i) camera that uses a bank of CCD units to capture an image and store it digitally on to a miniature disk or in RAM in the camera's body; (ii) video camera that stores images in digital form - the light from the image is converted into thousands of individual pixesl which store the intensity of the light at that point as a number, using either a light-sensitive cell or CCD unit; in a colour camera there are three sets of CCD units, each of which detects a particular colour and generates a value for each pixel representing the red, green and blue colours

see also
PHOTO-CD

digital cassette

high quality magnetic tape housed in a standard size cassette with write protect tabs, and a standard format leader

digital channel

communications path that can only transmit data as digital signals; voice, image or video signals have to be converted from analog to digital form before they can be transmitted over a digital channel

see also
A/D CONVERTER

digital clock

clock which shows the time as a series of digits (such as 12:22:04)

digital compact cassette (DCC)

magnetic tape in a compact cassette box that is used to store computer data or audio signals in a digital format (DCC is the newer version of the traditional audio cassette, but it has CD quality sound with the digital storage)

digital computer

computer which processes data in digital form (that is data represented in discrete digital form)
compare
ANALOG

digital data

data represented in (usually binary) numerical form

digital display

video display that can only show a fixed number of colours or shades of grey

digital monitor

video monitor that can only show a fixed number of colours or shades of grey; the monitor accepts a digital signal from the display adapter in the computer and converts it into an analog signal; examples are MDA, CGA and EGA monitors
compare with
ANALOG MONITOR

digital optical recording (DOR)

recording signals in binary form as small holes in the surface of an optical or compact disc which can then be read by laser

digital nonlinear editing

See
NONLINEAR VIDEO EDITING

digital plotter

plotter whose pen position is controllable in discrete steps, so that drawings in the computer can be output graphically

digital recording

see
DIGITAL VIDEO, NONLINEAR VIDEO EDITING, MAGNETIC RECORDING

digital resolution

smallest number that can be represented with one digit, the value assigned to the least significant bit of a word or number

digital signal

electric signal that has only a number of possible states, as opposed to analog signals which are continuously variable

digital signal processor (DSP)

special processor that carries out mathematical calculations on digital signals which have been converted from original analog signals (such as voice, audio or video); this type of processor is now used in telecommunications, voice processing, multimedia applications and modems

digital signalling

control and dialling codes sent down a (telephone line) in digital form

digital signature

unique identification code sent by a terminal or device in digital form, often used as a means of confirming the authenticity of a message or instruction

digital speech

see
SPEECH SYNTHESIS

digital to analog converter *or* D/A converter (DAC)

circuit that converts a digital signal to an analog one (the analog signal is proportional to the input binary number)

digital video

video recorded in digital form; the output from a video camera is converted to digital form using either a digital camera or a frame grabber - the digital output is then normally compressed before being processed or transmitted or stored on videotape

digital video effects

see
DVE

Digital Video Interactive™ (DV-I)

system that defines how video and audio signals should be compressed onto disk and then decompressed during playback on a computer; the DV-I technology is currently produced by Intel as a chip-set which can record or playback compressed full-motion video in real time

digitize

to change analog movement or signals into a digital form which can be processed by computers, etc.

digitized photograph

image or photograph that has been scanned to produce an analog signal which is then converted to digital form and stored or displayed on a computer

digitizing pad *or* tablet

sensitive surface that translates the position of a pen into numerical form, so that drawings can be entered into a computer

DIM

DOCUMENT IMAGE MANAGEMENT

software that allows a user to capture, store and index printed text in a digital form

DIN

DEUTSCHE INDUSTRIENORM

German industry standards organization; often refers to specification for plugs and sockets

Dingbat™

font that contains stars, bullets, symbols, images and drawings in place of characters, designed by Zapf

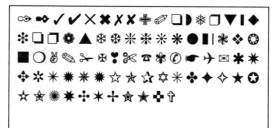

Dingbat symbol font

diode

electronic component that allows an electrical current to pass in one direction and not the other; for example, a light-emitting diode (LED) is a semiconductor diode that emits light when a current is applied (used in clock and calculator displays, and as an indicator)

DIP
DOCUMENT IMAGE PROCESSING
software that allows a user to capture, store and index printed text in a digital form

DIP
DUAL-IN-LINE PACKAGE
standard layout for integrated circuit packages using two parallel rows of connecting pins along each side

DIR
DIRECTORY
(in MS-DOS) system command that displays a list of files stored on a disk

direct data entry (DDE)
keying in data directly onto a magnetic disk or tape

direct graphics interface standard
see
DGIS

direct image
image that is composed directly onto the screen rather than being composed off-screen in memory before it is displayed; some authoring tools let you set an object's property so that you can choose whether it is drawn directly to screen or first drawn off-screen then transferred into the screen's memory area

direct memory access
see
DMA

Director™
multimedia authoring software developed by Macromedia that uses a grid to allow a user to control elements over time

directory
(in DOS and OS/2) method of organising the files stored on a disk; a directory can contain a group of files or further sub-directories

disc
flat circular plate that can contain data as tiny holes, read by a laser; disk normally refers to magnetic storage, wheras disc refers to optical storage

see also
CD-ROM

discrete multi-tone
see
DMT

disk
flat circular plate coated with a substance that is capable of being magnetized (data is stored on this by magnetizing selective sections to represent binary digits); disk normally refers to magnetic storage, wheras disc refers to optical storage
see also
FLOPPY DISK

disk controller
IC or circuits used to translate a request for data by the CPU into control signals for the disk drive (including motor control and access arm movement)

disk crash
fault caused by the read/write head touching the surface of the disk

disk drive
device that spins a magnetic disk and controls the position of the read/write head

disk operating system (DOS)
section of the operating system software that controls disk and file access

diskette
light, flexible disk that can store data in a magnetic form, used in most personal computers

diskless (workstation)
(workstation) which does not have any disk drives for data storage

display
device on which information or images can be presented visually

display adapter
device which allows information in a computer to be displayed on a CRT (the adapter interfaces with both the computer and CRT)

display attribute
variable which defines the shape or size or colour of text or graphics displayed

display character
graphical symbol which appears as a printed or displayed item, such as one of the letters of the alphabet or a number

display cycle
operations required to display an image on screen

display device
see
VIDEO DISPLAY BOARD

display element
(i) (in graphics) a basic graphic component, such as a background, foreground, text or graphics image; (ii) (in computer graphics) any component of an image

Display PostScript™
an extension of PostScript that allows PostScript commands to be interpreted and displayed on screen so that a user can see exactly what will appear on the printer

dissolve
transition effect between two scenes or audio segments in which one fades out as the second fades in

distort
to introduce unwanted differences between a signal input and output from a device

distortion
unwanted differences in a signal before and after it has passed through a piece of equipment

dither
(i) to create a curve or line that looks smoother by adding shaded pixels beside the pixels that make up the image; (ii) to create the appearance of a new colour by a pattern of coloured pixels that appear, to the eye, to combine and form a new, composite colour (for example, a pattern of black and white dots will appear like grey)

78

dithered colour

colour that is made up of a pattern of different coloured pixels

DLL

DYNAMIC LINK LIBRARY

(in Microsoft Windows and OS/2) library of utility programs that can be called from a main program when needed and when the program is running; this saves loading into memory functions that are only occasionally used

DLL file

file containing a library of routines that can be used by another program when required during the program's execution

DMA

DIRECT MEMORY ACCESS

direct, rapid link between a peripheral and a computer's main memory which avoids asking the processor to carry out retrieval from memory for each item of data required and so speeds up data transfer to and from main memory and a peripheral

DMA controller

interface IC that controls high-speed data transfer between a high-speed peripheral and main memory, usually the controller will also halt or cycle steal from the CPU

DMA cycle stealing

CPU allowing the DMA controller to send data over the bus during clock cycles when it performs internal or NOP instructions

DMT

DISCRETE MULTI-TONE

technology that uses digital signal processors to transmit video, sound, image and data over cable at high speed

document image management (DIM) *or* processing (DIP)

software that allows a user to capture, store and index printed text in a digital form

document interchange architecture/document content architecture

see
DIA/DCA

documentation
printed instruction or manual provided with hardware or software

dolly
trolley on wheels used to hold and move a camera smoothly

dongle
coded circuit or chip that has to be present in a system before a piece of copyright software will run

DOR
see
DIGITAL OPTICAL RECORDING

DOS
DISK OPERATING SYSTEM
section of the operating system software, that controls the disk and file access

dot
small round spot, such as one which makes up an image
see also
BITMAP

dot addressable
display adapter that allows software to control each pixel (or dot) on the display

dot command
method of writing instructions with a full stop followed by the command, used mainly for embedded commands in word-processor systems

dot matrix
method of forming characters by use of dots inside a rectangular matrix

dot-matrix printer
printer in which the characters are made up by a series of closely spaced dots (it produces a page line by line; a dot-matrix printer can be used either for printing using a ribbon or for thermal or electrostatic printing)

dots per inch *or* d.p.i. *or* dpi
standard method used to describe the resolution capabilities of a page printer or scanner

80

dot pitch

the vertical distance between the centre of two similar-coloured phosphor dots on a colour screen (for example, the distance between two adjacent red phosphor dots); the smaller the distance between the dots, the sharper the image displayed; typically the dot pitch is between .20 to .40mm

dot prompt

(in dBASE programming language) command prompt displayed as a single dot on screen

double-click

to click twice, rapidly, on a mouse button to start an action

double frequency scanning

(in CD-i) method of doubling the vertical resolution of a monitor by scanning at twice the normal rate

double speed

high speed at which a CD-ROM disc is spun by a drive, normally 460rpm

double strike

printing a character twice in order to make it appear bolder

DPI

DOTS PER INCH

standard method used to describe the resolution capabilities of a page printer or scanner

drag

to move (a mouse) while holding the button down, so moving an image or icon on screen

drag and drop

feature of some GUIs (including OS/2, Windows and System 7) in which a user can drag a section of text or icon or object onto another program icon; this starts the program and loads the data that was dragged onto it

drag image

the cursor, icon or outline image that is displayed when you drag an object across the screen

DRAM

DYNAMIC RANDOM ACCESS MEMORY

draw direct

process of drawing an object directly to the screen rather than to an off-screen memory buffer

drawing program

software that allows the user to draw and design on screen
see also
PAINT PROGRAM

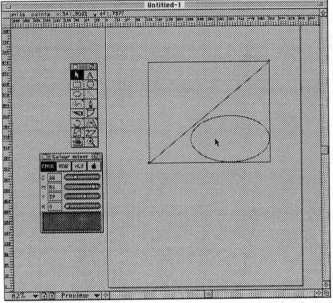

Drawing program allows shaps and line drawings to be accurately designed.

drawing tools

range of functions in a paint program that allows the user to draw; normally displayed as icons in a toolbar, the drawing tools might include a circle-draw, line-draw and freehand drawing tools

drive

mechanical device in a computer which operates a tape or disk, spinning the disk to the correct speed and moving the read/write head to the correct location under software control

driver *or* device driver *or* device handler
program or routine used to interface and manage an input/output device or other peripheral

DRO
DESTRUCTIVE READOUT
form of storage medium that loses its data after it has been read

drop-down list box
list of options for an entry that appears below a field when you move the cursor over the entry field

drop-down menu
menu of options that is displayed below a menu option when the user selects the menu option from the menu bar

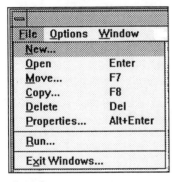

Drop-down menu displays options below the menu bar.

drop in
small piece of dirt that is on the surface of a disk or tape surface, which does not allow data to be recorded on that section

drop out
failure of a small piece of tape or disk to be correctly magnetized so it is unable to accurately store data

drum plotter
computer output device which consists of a movable pen and a piece of paper around a drum that can be rotated, creating patterns and text when both are moved in various ways

DSP
DIGITAL SIGNAL PROCESSOR

special processor that carries out mathematical calculations on digital signals which have been converted from original analog signals (such as voice, audio or video); this type of processor is now used in telecommunications, voice processing, multimedia applications and modems

DTP
DESKTOP PUBLISHING
the design, layout and printing of documents using special software, a desktop computer and a high-resolution printer; the software normally provides a WYSIWYG preview to show what the printed page will look like

DTV
see
DESKTOP VIDEO

dual-in-line package
see
DIP

dubbing
adding sound effects to a film or video

duration
length of time for which something lasts

DVE
DIGITAL VIDEO EFFECTS
special effects carried out by a PC on a video sequence; for example, a fade between two sequences or a dissolve

DV-I
DIGITAL VIDEO INTERACTIVE™
system that defines how video and audio signals should be compressed onto disk and then decompressed during playback on a computer; the DV-I technology is currently produced as a chip-set by Intel which can record or playback compressed full-motion video in real time

dye-polymer recording
(in optical disks) recording method which creates minute changes in a thin layer of dye imbedded in the plastic optical disk; dye-polymer recording has one big advantage - that the data stored on the optical disk using this method can be erased

dye-sublimation printer

high-quality colour printer that produces images by squirting tiny drops of coloured ink onto paper

dynamic allocation

system where resources are allocated during a program run, rather than being determined in advance

dynamic data exchange (DDE)

(in Microsoft Windows and OS/2) method in which two active programs can exchange data; one program asks the operating system to create a link between it and another program

dynamic link library (DLL)

(in Microsoft Windows and OS/2) library of utility programs that can be called from a main program when needed and when the program is running; this saves loading into memory functions that are only occasionally used

dynamic memory *or* dynamic RAM *or* DRAM

random access memory that requires its contents to be updated regularly

dynamic update

a display (such as a graph) updated in real time as new data arrives

DYUV

DELTA YUV

digital video encoding technique in which luminance of a pixel is calculated by the RGB input signal (Y0.6G + 0.3R + 0.1B); from the value of Y, U and V are calculated as UR - Y; VB - Y

Ee

EBF

ELECTRON BEAM RECORDING
recording the output from a computer directly onto microfilm using an electron beam

edge

side of a flat object or signal or clock pulse

edge detection

algorithm and routines used in graphics software to define the edges of an object, often used to convert a bitmap to a vector image or for special effects or to sharpen an image

edge-triggered

process or circuit which is clocked or synchronized by the changing level (edge) of a clock signal rather than the level itself

EDI

ELECTRONIC DATA INTERCHANGE
system of sending orders, paying invoices or transferring company information over a network or telephone line using an electronic mail system; often used to send instructions to pay money direct from one company to another, or from one bank to a company

edit key

key which starts a function that makes an editor easier to use

edit window

area of the screen in which the user can display and edit text or graphics

edit decision list (EDL)

off-line video editing method in which the operator defines the points where he would like the video to be edited; this list of actions is then used in an on-line edit suite to carry out the edits automatically
See also
NONLINEAR VIDEO EDITING

EDP

ELECTRONIC DATA PROCESSING
data processing using computers and electronic devices

EDTV

EXTENDED-DEFINITION TELEVISION
enhancement to the NTSC standard for television transmission that offers higher definition and a wide aspect ratio; EDTV normally has an aspect ratio of 4:3; if greater than this, the standard is called EDTV-wide

edutainment

software that is a cross between entertainment (or games software) and educational products

EEMS

ENHANCED EXPANDED MEMORY SYSTEM
(in an IBM PC) development of EMS; standard method of expanding the main memory fitted into a PC
see also
EMS

EEPROM

ELECTRICALLY ERASABLE PROGRAMMABLE READ-ONLY MEMORY
storage chip which can be programmed and erased using electrical signals

EGA

ENHANCED GRAPHICS ADAPTER
(in an IBM PC) popular standard for medium-resolution colour graphics display at a maximum resolution of 640x350 pixels; an EGA graphics adapter requires a digital RGB monitor to display the images

87

see also
CGA, VGA
for PC graphics, see also
APPENDIX

EISA
ELECTRONICS INDUSTRY STANDARDS ASSOCIATION
group of PC manufacturers who formed an association to promote a 32-bit expansion bus standard as a rival to the MCA bus standard from IBM; the EISA expansion bus standard is backwards compatible with the older ISA standard of expansion cards, but also features 32-bit data path and allows bus mastering.

either-or operation
logical function that produces a true output if any input is true

elastic banding
method of defining the limits of an image on a computer screen by stretching a boundary around it

elastic buffer
buffer size that changes its size according to demand

electically erasable read-only memory
see
EEPROM

electroluminescent display
flat, lightweight display screen made up of two pieces of glass covered with a grid of conductors, separated by a thin layer of gas which luminesces when a point of the grid is selected by two electric signals

electron beam recording (EBR)
recording the output from a computer directly onto microfilm using an electron beam

Electronic Arts™
largest publisher of interactive software including console games, PC and Macintosh titles

electronic book
term that describes a multimedia title

electronic data interchange
see
EDI

electronic data processing (EDP)
data processing using computers and electronic devices

Electronic Industry Standards Association
see
EISA

electronic mail *or* email *or* e-mail
system of sending messages to and receiving messages from other users on a network

electronic mailbox
area or directory on a disk used to store messages sent by electronic mail until the person to whom they were sent is ready to read them

electronic pen *or* stylus *or* wand
light pen or wand; stylus used to draw on a graphics tablet

electronic publishing
(i) use of desktop publishing packages and laser printers to produce printed matter; (ii) using computers to create and display information, such as viewdata

electronic pulse
short voltage pulse

electronic shopping
system of shopping from the home, using computerized catalogues displayed on television or on a computer; software lets you view the goods and pay by credit card, all by means of a home computer terminal and a modem or interactive television

electronic smog
excessive stray electromagnetic fields and static electricity generated by large numbers of electronic devices (this can damage equipment or sometimes even a person's health)

electronic traffic
data transmitted in the form of electronic pulses

electrophotographic

printing technique used in many laser printers in which a laser beam creates an image on a charged drum; this then attracts particles of fine black toner, the drum transfers the image to the paper which is then heated to melt the toner onto the paper

electrosensitive paper

metal-coated printing paper which can display characters using localized heating with a special dot-matrix print head

elegant programming

writing a well-structured program using the minimum number of instructions so that the program is easy to understand and runs efficiently

elevator

small, square indicator displayed within a scroll bar that indicates where you are within a long document or image; the user can scroll through the image or text by dragging the elevator up or down the scroll bar

em

measure equal to the width of the letter `m' in a particular font

E-mail *or* email

ELECTRONIC MAIL

system of sending messages to and receiving messages from other users on a network

embedded code

sections or routines written in machine code, inserted into a high-level program to speed up or perform a special function

embedded command

printer command (such as indicating that text should be in italic) inserted into the text and used by a word-processing system when producing formatted printed text

embedded object

(in Windows) feature of OLE that allows a file or object - such as an image - that is included within another document or file; unlike linking, in which a link to the file or object is included

see

OLE

90

embedding

(in Windows) to drag an object and drop it into a document or file so that is is embedded within the document
see
OLE

EMM

EXPANDED MEMORY MANAGER
software driver which manages the extra expanded memory fitted in an IBM PC and makes it available for programs to use

emphasis

(i) filter that helps cut down the background noise and so boost a signal; (ii) special effects function in a paint program that will increase the value of a range of colours so that they appear brighter

EMS *or* LIM EMS

EXPANDED MEMORY SYSTEM *OR* LOTUS-INTEL-MICROSOFT EXPANDED MEMORY SYSTEM
(in an IBM PC) standard that defines extra memory added above the 640Kb limit of conventional memory; this memory can only be used by specially written programs

emulate

to copy something or behave like something else

emulation

behaviour by one computer or printer which is exactly the same as another, and which allows the same programs to be run and the same data to be processed

emulation facility

feature of hardware or software which emulates another system

emulator

software or hardware that allows a machine to behave like another

emulsion laser storage

digital storage technique using a laser to expose light sensitive material

en

unit of measure equal to half the width of an em

enabled

menu option, button or hotspot that will carry out a function if selectd by a user; when a menu option is not enabled it appears grey and cannot be selected

encapsulated

(something) contained within something else

encapsulated PostScript *or* EPS

PostScript commands that describe an image or page that are contained within a file; the encapsulated PostScript file can be placed within a graphics image or DTP page; an encapsulated PostScript file often contains a preview bitmap image of the page in TIFF or PICT format that can be easily displayed by a graphics application

encapsulated PostScript file (EPSF)

file that contains encapsulated PostScript instructions together with a preview bitmap image

encode

to convert data into a (normally more compact) coded form

encoder

(in video) electronic device that converts a video signal made up of separate signals (such as RGB) into a composite video signal

enclosed object

graphic object that is closed on all sides and so can be filled with a colour or pattern

end of file (EOF)

character in a file that indicates the end of the file

end user

person who will use the device or program or product

engine

library of software routines optimised to perform a particular task, such as database search or graphics display; in a multimedia application, the front-end is often produced using a high-level programming language that is easy to use, but slow, and the database or display routines are written in a separate engine in low-level code for speed

enhanced expanded memory specification (EEMS)

(in an IBM PC) a development of EMS, the standard method of expanding the main memory fitted into a PC

enhanced graphics adapter (EGA)

(in an IBM PC) popular standard for medium-resolution colour graphics display at a maximum resolution of 640x350 pixels; an EGA graphics adapter requires a digital RGB monitor to display the images
see also
CGA, VGA
>APPENDIX: PC GRAPHICS MODES

enhanced graphics adapter screen

digital high-resolution colour monitor that can display EGA system signals and graphics

enhanced keyboard

(in an IBM PC) keyboard with 101 or 102 keys and a row of 12 function keys arranged along the top of the keyboard, with a separate numeric keypad on the right

enhanced small device interface (ESDI)

interface standard between a CPU and peripherals such as disk drives; NOTE: this standard is no longer commonly used and has been replaced by the SCSI standard
see also
IDE, SCSI

enhanced mode

(in an IBM PC with an Intel 80386 CPU) operation of software which uses the CPU's protected mode to allow several MS-DOS programs to run in a multitasking environment

envelope

shape of the curve of a sound over time

environment space

the amount of memory free to be used by a program

environment variable

variable set by the system or by a user at the system command line which can be used by any program

EOF
END OF FILE

EPROM
ERASABLE PROGRAMMABLE READ-ONLY MEMORY

EPS
ENCAPSULATED POSTSCRIPT

EPSF
ENCAPSULATED POSTSCRIPT FILE

erasable programmable read-only memory (EPROM)
read-only memory chip that can be programmed by sending data to the chip and, at the same time, applying a voltage to the write pin; usually erasable by exposing to ultra-violet light

erase
(i) to set all the digits in a storage area to zero; (ii) to remove any signal from a magnetic medium; (iii) tool in a graphics program that sets an area of an image to the same colour as the background

erase head
small magnet that clears a magnetic tape or disk of recorded signals

erase character
character which means 'do nothing'

eraser tool
(in a graphics program) function that allows areas of an image to be erased, or set to the background colour

ergonomics
science of designing software or hardware so that it is comfortable and safe to use

error
mistake due to an operator; mistake caused by a hardware or software fault; mistake in a program that prevents a program or system running correctly

error box
dialog box displayed with a message alerting the user that an error has occurred

error code
code which indicates that a particular type of error has occurred

error condition
state that is entered if an attempt is made to operate on data containing errors

error message
report displayed to the user saying that an error has occurred

ESDI
ENHANCED SMALL DEVICE INTERFACE
interface standard between a CPU and peripherals such as disk drives; NOTE: this standard is no longer commonly used and has been replaced by the SCSI standard

Ethernet
(refers to IEEE 802.3 standard) standard defining the protocol and signalling method of a local area network; thick-Ethernet uses thick coaxial cable and transceivers to connect branch cables and can stretch over long distances; by contrast, a thin-Ethernet (the most popular type of Ethernet) network is implemented using thin coaxial cable and BNC connectors and is limited to distances of around 1000m; normally transmits data at 10Mbps
compare
ARCNET, TOKEN-RING

EtherTalk
(in Apple Macintosh systems) variation of the standard Ethernet network developed to connect Macintosh computers together as an alternative to the slower AppleTalk

evaluate
to calculate the answer to an expression

evaluation copy
demonstration version of a software product that lets you try the main functions of a software product before buying it

event
an action or activity

event-driven
(computer program or process) where each step of the execution relies on external actions

event handler

routine that responds to an event or message within an object-oriented programming environment; for example, if a user clicks the mouse button this generates a message which can be acted upon by the event handler

EXE file

(in DOS or OS/2 operating systems) three-letter extension to a filename which indicates that the file contains binary data of a program; the file can be executed directly by the operating system

executable file

file that contains a program rather than data

executable form

program translated or compiled into a machine code form that a processor can execute

execute

to run or carry out a computer program or process

exit

to stop program execution or to leave a program and return control to the operating system or interpreter

EXIT

(in MS-DOS) system command to stop and leave a child process and return to the original process; for example, to quit and close a DOS session within MS Windows, type EXIT

exit point

point in a subroutine where control is returned to the main program

expanded memory manager (EMM)

software driver which manages the extra expanded memory fitted in an IBM PC and makes it available for programs to use

expanded memory system (EMS)

(in an IBM PC) standard that defines extra memory added above the 640Kb limit of conventional memory; this memory can only be used by specially-written programs
see also
LIM

expansion
increase in computing power or storage size

expansion box
device that plugs into an expansion bus and provides several more free expansion slots, normally used with a laptop to provide expansion connectors

expansion bus
data and address lines leading to a connector and allowing expansion cards to control and access the data in main memory

expansion card
add-in interface board that plugs into an expansion bus in a computer to either enhance the computer's memory or interface with another device (for example, a graphics expansion card provides an interface between a computer and a monitor)

expansion slot
connector in a computer that allows an expansion card to be plugged in to expand the system

expert system
software which applies the knowledge, advice and rules defined by experts in a particular field to a user's data to help solve a problem

explicit reference
(within a program or script) a way of identifying a particular object, such as a field or button, by a unique name

export
to save data in a different file format other than the software's default; for example, if you use Microsoft Word you would normally save the file as a DOC format file, if you want to use the Viewer authoring tool, you would need to export the document as an RTF format file

expression
definition of a variable or value in a program
compare with
CONTAINER

extended character set
symbols or foreign characters within a character set with an ASCII value between 128 and 255

extended-definition television (EDTV)
enhancement to the NTSC standard for television transmission that offers higher definition and a wider aspect ratio; EDTV normally has an aspect ratio of 4:3, if the broadcaster wants to provide a greater aspect ratio than this, the standard is called EDTV-wide

extended graphics array (XGA)
high resolution graphics standard developed by IBM; capable of displaying resolutions of up to 1024x768 pixels
>APPENDIX: PC GRAPHICS

extended industry standard architecture
see
EISA

extended level synthesizer
synthesizer on a sound card that supports nine melodic instruments and can play 16 notes simultaneously; waveform synthesizers are extended level synthesizers
compare with
BASE LEVEL SYNTHESIZER

extended memory
(in an IBM PC) most popular standard method of adding extra memory above the 1Mb point which can be used directly by many operating systems or programs

extended memory manager
software driver that configures extra memory fitted in a PC to conform to the extended memory standard

extended memory specification (XMS)
rules that define how a program should access extended memory fitted in a PC

extensible
software that can be extended by the user or by third-party software; normally refers to a product, such as Microsoft's At Work system, that allows programmers and manufacturers to add their own functions and drivers to support special hardware

extension
additional information after a filename, indicating the type or use of the file; in

MS-DOS and OS/2, there is a three-character filename extension that normally indicates the type of file; for example, a TIFF file has a .TIF extension, a sound file either a .WAV or .SND or .MDI extension and an application program either a .EXE or .COM extension

monoumb.386	more.com	drvspace.ex~
vfintd.386	sys.com	scandisk.ex~
dblspace.bat	tree.com	append.exe
defrag.bat	unformat.com	attrib.exe
drvspace.bat	vsafe.com	chkdsk.exe
scandisk.bat	ega.cpi	debug.exe
dblspace.bin	ega2.cpi	deltree.exe
drvspace.bin	ega3.cpi	dosshell.exe

In DOS, OS/2 and Unix, file names have a three-letter extension

fade

effect in which a sound or image (or part of an image) gradually gets weaker over a period of time; often used when changing between two images on screen

fade in

image that starts with a blank screen that gradually shows the image

fade out

image that gradually fades to a blank screen

family

(i) range of different designs of a particular typeface; (ii) range of machines from one manufacturer that are compatible with other products in the same line from the same manufacturer

FAT

FILE ALLOCATION TABLE

(in DOS, and some other operating systems) data file stored on disk that contains the names of each file stored on the disk, together with its starting sector position, date and size

FatBits™

MacPaint option which allows a user to edit an image one pixel at a time

FDM

FREQUENCY DIVISION MULTIPLEXING

assigning a number of different signals to different frequencies (or bands) to allow many signals to be sent along one channel

feedback

part of an output signal that is fed back to the input and amplified; normally an unwanted situation - for example, if a microphone is too close to a speaker the result is positive feedback or a howl

FED

see
FIELD EMISSION DISPLAY

field

(i) object on-screen that can contain text; fields can normally display stored or calculated text or accept user input; (ii) television image made up of every other line of the full picture; (iii) sections containing individual data items in a record

field emission display (FED)

method of producing thin, flat displays for laptop computers in which a miniature colour CRT is located at each pixel point; this method uses less energy and provides a sharper image than active matrix LCD colour screen

FIF

FRACTAL IMAGE FORMAT

file format used to store graphics images which have been highly-compressed using fractals

file

named section of a disk that contains data and can be accessed as a single unit

file allocation table (FAT)

(in DOS, and some other operating systems) data file stored on disk that contains the names of each file stored on the disk, together with its starting sector position, date and size

file attributes

control bits of data stored with each file which control particular functions or aspects of the file such as making it read-only, marking it ready to be archived or that it is a system file

file element
complete file contained within a RIFF compound file

file format
standard way in which information is stored within a file, for example a graphics image can be stored in many different ways according to the file format used
see also
TIFF, EPS, CGM

file locking
software mechanism that prevents data in a file being updated by two different users at the same time; only one user can change the particular information at any one time

fill
to draw an enclosed area in one colour or shading or pattern

film recorder
device that produces a 35mm slide from a computer image; a film recorder can produce slides at very high resolution, normally around 3,000 lines, by re-generating the image on an internal screen

filter
option in a software application that allows it to inport or export a particular foreign file type; for example, most graphics packages have import filters that will decode TIFF, BMP and PCX file formats

Finder™
(in an Apple Macintosh system) graphical user interface that is used to operate the Macintosh; allowing a user to view files, organise files into folders and start and control applications using a mouse

fine
very high resolution image or very small pixels

fine tune
to adjust by small amounts the features or parameters of hardware or software to improve performance

firmware
computer program or data that is permanently stored in a hardware memory chip, such as a ROM or EPROM

compare
HARDWARE, SOFTWARE

first fit
routine or algorithm that selects the first, largest section of free memory in which to store a (virtual) page

first generation image
master copy of an original image, text or document

fixed-field file
data file in which each field consists of a pre-defined and fixed number of characters; spaces are used to pad out each field to the correct length
compare with
DELIMITED-FIELD FILE

fixed-frequency monitor
monitor that can only accept one frequency and type of video signal, such as VGA-only monitor
compare with
MULTISCAN MONITOR.

flagging
putting an indicator against an item so that it can be found later
see also
BOOKMARK

flash
to switch a light on and off; to increase and lower the brightness of a cursor to provide an indicator

flash A/D
parallel high speed A/D converter

flash memory
non-volatile memory similar to an EEPROM device but which operates with blocks of data rather than single bytes; most often used as an alternative to a disk drive

flat screen
monitor tube that has a very flat display area with nearly square corners, rather than the usual tube with a curved display with rounded edges; a flat screen distorts an image less than a conventional CRT

flatbed

printing or scanning machine that holds the paper or image on a flat surface while processing

flatbed plotter

movable pen that draws diagrams under the control of a computer onto a flat piece of paper

flatbed scanner

device with a flat sheet of glass on which an image or photograph is placed; the scan head moves below the glass and converts the image into data wich can be manipulated by computer
see also
SCANNER

flicker

computer graphic image whose brightness alternates due to a low image refresh rate or signal corruption

flicker-free

(display) that does not flicker

floating window

window that can be moved anywhere on screen; often used to describe a toolbar that can be moved around

floppy disk *or* floppy *or* FD

secondary storage device, in the form of a flat, circular flexible disk onto which data can be stored in a magnetic form (a floppy disk cannot store as much data as a hard disk, but is easily removed, and is protected by a flexible paper or plastic sleeve); the current standards are 3 1/2-inch diameter disks which can store 720Kb or 1.44Mb of data or 5 1/4-inch disks which can store 360Kb or 1.2Mb. PCs and Macintosh computers normally use the 3 1/2-inch 1.44Mb standard (but with different formatting)

flow text

to insert text into a page format in a DTP system; the text fills all the space around pictures, and between set margins

flush

(i) to clear or erase all the contents of a queue, buffer, file or section of memory; (ii) level or in line with

flush buffers

to erase any data remaining in a buffer, ready for a new job or after a job has been aborted

flush left *or* flush right

see
LEFT JUSTIFY, RIGHT JUSTIFY

flutter

fluctuations of tape speed due to mechanical or circuit problems, causing signal distortion

flyback *or* line flyback

movement of an electron picture beam to return from the end of a scan to the beginning of the next scan

FM

FREQUENCY MODULATION

to vary the frequency of one signal according to the level of a second signal; sound synthesizers use FM synthesis to create a sound like an instrument, radio transmission uses frequency modulation in which avery high frequency carrier signal is modified in level by the sound to be transmitted
see also
WAVEFORM

FM synthesizer

synthesizer that generates sounds by combining base signals of different frequencies
compare with
WAVEFORM SYNTHESIZER

focus

(i) to adjust a CRT so that the displayed image appears clearer and sharper; (ii) an object that is currently accepting user input or is being controlled by a program and accepting commands from the program (for example, a button or check-box on screen)

focus window

window in a GUI that is currently active and accepting user input or is being controlled by a program and accepting commands from the program (for example, if a user selects the window or if the program changes the background colour of the window)

105

folder

(in an Apple Macintosh) location for a group of files stored together under a
name, similar to a directory under MS-DOS; to open a folder and see the files
it contains, double click on the folder's icon
see also
DIRECTORY

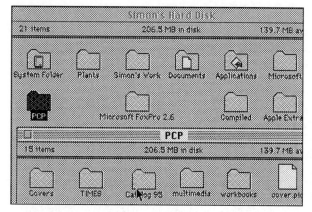

*In a
Macintosh,
folders are
displayed
graphically.*

font *or* fount

set of characters all of the same style, size and typeface

font card

ROM device that fits into a socket on a printer and adds another resident font

font change

function on a computer to change the style of characters used on a display
screen

Font/DA Mover

(in an Apple Macintosh system) system utility that allows a user to add fonts
and DA files to the system environment

font disk

magnetic disk that contains the data to drive a character generator to make up
the various fonts on a computer display

footer

text at the bottom of all the pages in a document (such as the page number)

footnote

note at the bottom of a page, which refers to particular text in the page above it, usually using a superior number as a reference

foreground

(i) front part of an illustration (as opposed to the background); (ii) image displayed in front of another image in a video clip (for example, Windows Movie Player displays an object in a high score channel in front of an object in a low score channel)

foreground colour

colour of characters and text displayed on a screen

fork

(in an Apple Machintosh) special folder that contains system files and information about a file or application

form

(i) preprinted document with blank spaces where information can be entered; (ii) graphical display that looks like an existing printed form and is used to enter data into a database

form type

four-character code that identifies the type of data chunk within a RIFF file (for example, WAVE means waveform data)

format

to arrange text as it will appear in printed form on paper

format a disk

(i) to set up a blank disk so that it is ready for data, by writing control and track location information on it; (ii) to define the areas of a disk reserved for data and control

fourcc

FOUR-CHARACTER CODE
method of identifying the type of data within a RIFF file

fps

FRAMES PER SECOND
number of individual images (or frames) that can be displayed each second to give the impression of movement; for example, TV displays 25 frames per second which is fast enough to appear as continuous movement to the eye

fractal

geometric shape that repeats itself within itself and always appears the same, however much you magnify the image

fractal compression

technique used to compress images; uses complex alogrithms to store images as fractals and so offers very high data compression of up to 200:1 using fractal algorithms to represent an image

fractal image format (FIF)

file format used to store graphics images which have been highly-compressed using fractals

fragmentation

(on a disk drive) files stored scattered across non-contiguous sectors on a hard disk; when a file is saved to disk, it is not always saved in adjacent sectors; this will increase the retrieval time. Defragmentation moves files back into adjacent sectors so that the read head does not have to move far across the disk, so it increases performance.

frame

(i) one complete image displayed on a television screen (in the US this is made up of 525 lines, in the UK it is 625 lines); (ii) one screen of data; (iii) (in DTP) a movable, resizable box that holds text or an image; (iv) one complete image within a video or animation sequence

frame-based animation

series of screens displayed in quick succession, each one slightly different, that gives the impression of movement
compare with
CAST-BASED

frame buffer

section of memory used to store an image before it is displayed on screen

frame grabber

high speed digital sampling circuit that stores a single frame of a TV transmission or full-motion video sequence in memory so that it can then be processed

frame hook

function executed by the Windows Movie Player for each frame of the video

frame index

variable used by the Movie Player that identifies the current frame of the video

frame rate

speed at which frames in a video sequence are displayed; measured in frames (one still image) displayed per second; PAL is 25fps, NTSC is 30fps and film is 24fps

frame window

controls (including the minimise and maximise buttons, scroll bar and window title) and border that surround a window area

freeze frame

to stop a video playback sequence so that only one frame is displayed as a fixed image

frequency division multiplexing (FDM)

assigning a number of different signals to different frequencies (or bands) to allow many signals to be sent along one channel

frequency modulation (FM)

see
FM

friendly front-end

design of the display of a program that is easy to use and understand

front-end

display presented by a program that is seen by an end user

full motion video

transmission of video or television data that is displayed in real time and shows smooth, continuous movement rather than single frame or jerky movements; it needs a computer fitted with a digitising card that is fast enough to capture and display moving video images (PAL video is displayed at 25fps, NTSC at 30fps and film at 24fps)
Compare with
FREEZE FRAME.

full-screen

(program display) that uses all the available screen; it is not displayed within a window

full-text search

to carry out a search for something through all the text in a file or database rather than limiting the search to an area or field within a database

function

(i) mathematical formula, where a result is dependent upon several other numbers; (ii) sequence of computer program instructions in a main program that perform a certain task

function key *or* programmable function key

key or switch that has been assigned a particular task or sequence of instructions; COMMENT: function keys often form a separate group of keys on the keyboard, and have specific functions attached to them. On a PC's keyboard there are 12 function keys located in a row above the main characters and labelled F1, F2, etc.

fuzzy logic *or* fuzzy theory

type of logic applied to computer programming, which tries to replicate the reasoning methods of the human brain

Gg

G
GIGA

meaning one thousand million; in computing G refers to 230 , equal to 1,073,741,824

GaAs
GALLIUM ARSENIDE

gain
increase or becoming larger; amount by which a signal amplitude is changed as it passes through a circuit, usually given as a ratio of output to input amplitude

gallium arsenide (GaAs)
substance used to manufcature high-speed integrated circuit chips, an alternative to silicon

game paddle
device held in the hand to move a cursor or graphics in a computer game

game port
connection that allows a joystick to be plugged into a computer

games console
dedicated computer, joystick and display adapter that is designed to be only

used to play games

gap loss
signal attenuation due to incorrect alignment of the read/write head with the storage medium (such as magnetic tape)

garbage
(i) radio interference between adjacent analog or digital channels; (ii) data or information that is no longer required because it is out of date or contains errors

garbage in garbage out
see
GIGO

gas discharge display *or* gas plasma display
flat, lightweight display screen that is made of two flat pieces of glass covered with a grid of conductors, separated by a thin layer of a gas which luminesces when one point of the grid is selected by two electric signals
see also
LCD

generation loss
degradation of signal quality with each successive recording of a video or audio signal

generator lock
see
GENLOCK

General MIDI
standards for a synthesizer that set out the first 128 different instrument sounds in a synthesizer and the patch number that refers to it; for example, patch 40 is always a violin

generic
(something) that is compatible with a whole family of hardware or software devices from one manufacturer

genlock
GENERATOR LOCK
device that synchronizes two video signals from different sources so that they can be successfully combined or mixed; often used to synchronise the output

of a computer's display adapter with an external video source when using the computer to create overlays or titling

ghost

(i) (fault) video signal that displays a second, faint image beside the main image on a screen; (ii) sometimes used to mean 'greyed' menu items that are displayed in grey and are not currently available

GHz

GIGAHERTZ

GIF

GRAPHICS INTERFACE FORMAT

graphics file format of a file containing a bit-mapped image; originally used on the CompuServe on-line system, now a standard for encoding colour bit-mapped images normally in either 16 or 256 colours with options for compression

giga (G)

meaning one thousand million; in computing G refers to 2^{30} , equal to 1,073,741,824

gigabyte

10^9 bytes; in computing giga refers to 2^{30}, which is equal to 1,073,741,824

gigahertz (GHz)

frequency of one thousand million cycles per second

GIGO

GARBAGE IN GARBAGE OUT

expression meaning that the accuracy and quality of information that is output depends on the quality of the input; COMMENT: GIGO is sometimes taken to mean 'garbage in gospel out': i.e. that whatever wrong information is put into a computer, people will always believe that the output results are true

GKS

GRAPHICS KERNEL SYSTEM

standard for software command and functions describing graphical input/output to provide the same functions, etc. on any type of hardware

glare

very bright light reflections, especially on a VDU screen

glare filter
coated glass or plastic sheet placed in front of a screen to cut out bright light reflections

glitch
anything which causes the sudden unexpected failure of a computer or equipment

global
meaning which covers everything

global variable
variable or number that can be accessed by any routine or structure in a program
compare
LOCAL VARIABLE

global memory
(in Microsoft Windows) memory available to all Windows applications

gold contacts
electrical contacts, (usually for low-level signals) that are coated with gold to reduce the electrical resistance

grabber
high speed digital sampling circuit that stores a TV picture in memory so that it can then be processed by a computer

granularity
size of memory segments in a virtual memory system, such as Microsoft Windows

graphic display resolution
number of pixels that a computer is able to display on the screen

graphic object
small graphic image imported from another drawing application and placed on a page; in most DTP, paint or drawing packages, the object can be moved, sized and positioned independently from the other elements on the page

graphical user interface
see
GUI

graphics

pictures or lines which can be drawn on paper or on a screen to represent information

graphics accelerator

video display board with its own graphics coprocessor and high-speed RAM that can carry out graphical drawing operations (such as fill) at high speed; often used to speed up GUIs such as Windows or for graphics-intensive applications such as multimedia or DTP

graphics adapter

electronic device (normally on an expansion card) in a computer that converts software commands into electrical signals that display graphics on a connected monitor

graphics character

preprogrammed shape that can be displayed on a non-graphical screen instead of a character, used extensively in videotext systems to display simple pictures

graphics coprocessor

see
GRAPHICS PROCESSOR

graphics file

(binary) file which contains data describing an image

graphics file format

method in which data describing an image is stored
see also
GIF, PCX, PICT, TIFF

graphics kernel system (GKS)

standard for software command and functions describing graphical input/output to provide the same functions etc. on any type of hardware

graphics library

number of routines stored in a library file that can be added to any user program to simplify the task of writing graphics programs

graphics mode

videotext terminal whose displayed characters are taken from a range of graphics characters instead of text

graphics overlay card

expansion card for a PC or Macintosh that combines generated text or images with an external video source

graphics pad *or* tablet

flat device that allows a user to input graphical information into a computer by drawing on its surface

graphics primitive

basic shape (such as an arc, line or filled square) that is used to create other shapes or objects

graphics printer

printer capable of printing bit-mapped images

graphics processor *or* graphics coprocessor

secondary processor used to speed up the display of graphics: it calculates the position of pixels that form a line or shape and display graphic lines or shapes

graphics software

prewritten routines which perform standard graphics commands such as line drawing, plotting, etc., that can be called from within a program to simplify program writing

graphics terminal

special terminal with a high-resolution graphic display and graphics pad or other input device

graphics: vector and raster

there are two methods generally used to store an image: vector graphics (also known as object-oriented graphics), stores the image as a series of points, lines, arcs and other geometric shapes; raster graphics (or bitmap graphics) represents the image as a grid of pixels or dots; paint packages generally let you work on bitmap graphics, a drawing package or CAD software uses vector graphics

gray scale

see
GREY SCALE

greeked

(in a DTP program) font with a point size too small to display accurately, shown as a line rather than individual characters; thumbnail displays of a page or image use greeked text to give a representation of the final layout

Green Book
formal specification for CD-i standard published by Philips
see also
CD-I, RED BOOK, WHITE BOOK,YELLOW BOOK

grey scale
shades of grey between black and white; a line drawing has no grey scale information, only black or white; a scanner will scan a photograph with grey levels representing the tones; like colour information, a grey scale needs multiple bits of data for each pixel - 256 grey scales per pixel requires one byte (8 bits)
see also
HALFTONE

grid
matrix of non-printing lines which help align images or drawings on screen

grid snap
(in a graphics program) feature that limits the position of the cursor to a point on the grid, so ensuring that drawings are aligned

group
collection of objects that can be moved or resized as a single object

GUI
GRAPHICAL USER INTERFACE
interface between an operating system or program and the user; it uses graphics or icons to represent functions or files and allow the software to be controlled more easily; system commands do not have to be typed in; GUIs normally use a combination of windows, icons and a mouse to control the operating system. In many GUIs, such as Microsoft Windows, Apple Macintosh System 7, you can control all the functions of the operating system just using the mouse. Icons represent programs and files; instead of entering the file name, you select it by moving a pointer with a mouse.
compare
COMMAND LINE INTERFACE

gutter
(i) space between two adjacent columns of text; (ii) blank space or inner margin between two facing pages

Hh

H & J
HYPHENATION AND JUSTIFICATION

hairline rule
(in a DTP system) very thin line

halftone
photograph or image that originally had continuous tones, now displayed or printed using groups of dots to represent the tones; small dots represent lighter tones and larger dots the darker tones - halftones are produced before printing since printers (laser and offset) can only print dots or line drawings

hand-held scanner
device that is held in your hand and contains a row of phot-electic cells which, when moved over an image, convert it into data which can be displayed as an image on a computer

handle
(i) (in programming) number used to identify an active file within the program that is accessing the file; (ii) (in a GUI) small square displayed on a frame around an object or image that a user can select and drag to change the shape of the frame or graphical object

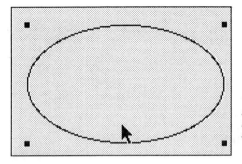

This graphc object has been selected and displays four handles to allow a user to stretch or distort the object

handler

(i) set of commands that are associated with an object and are executed when a user selects the object; for example, a series of commands that define what happens when a user clicks on a button; (ii) special software routine that controls a device or function
see also
DEVICE DRIVER

handwriting recognition

feature of software that is capable of recognising handwritten text and converting it into ASCII characters

hang

to enter an endless loop and not respond to further instruction

hard copy

printed document or copy of information contained in a computer or system, in a form that is readable (as opposed to soft copy)

hard disk

rigid magnetic disk that is able to store many times more data than a floppy disk, and usually cannot be removed from the disk drive; hard disk drives are normally compact (3.5-inch diameter) and offer low access times (around 15ms) and high capacity (normal is 120Mb)

hard reset

switch or signal that contols the CPU and resets the processor and any attached devices to their initial condition, equivalent to switching the computer off then back on again

hardware
physical units, components, integrated circuits, disks and mechanisms that make up a computer or its peripherals

hardware compatibility
architecture of two different computers that allows one to run the programs of the other without changing any device drivers or memory locations, or the ability of one to use the add-on boards of the other

hardware configuration
way in which the hardware of a computer system is connected together and configured

hardware dependent
something which will only work with a particular model or brand of computer hardware

hash code
numeric code that identifies an entry (in an index), produced by a hashing function

hashing function
algorithm used to produce a hash code for an entry and ensure that it is different from every other entry

HDTV
HIGH DEFINITION TELEVISION

head
transducer that can read or write data from the surface of a magnetic storage medium, such as a magnetic tape or floppy disk

head alignment
(i) correct position of a tape or disk head in relation to the magnetic surface, to give the best performance and correct track location; (ii) location of the read head in the same position as the write head was (in relation to the magnetic medium)

head of form
first line on a form or sheet of paper that can be printed on

header
(i) text that appears at the top of every page; (ii) words at the top of a page of

a document (such as title, author's name, page number, etc.)
see also
FOOTER

heading

(i) title or name of a document or file; (ii) header or words at the top of each page of a document (such as the title, the page numbers, etc.); (iii) title for a page within a multimedia book

heap

temporary data storage area that allows random access
compare
STACK

helical scan

method of storing data on magnetic tape in which the write head stores data in diagonal strips rather than parallel with the tape edge using the tape area more efficiently and allowing more data to be recorded; used most often in video tape recorders

help

function in a program or system that provides useful information about the program in use; context-sensitive help provides useful information about the particular function or part of the program you are in, rather than general information about the whole program; most software applications for IBM PCs have standardized the use of the F1 function key to display help text explaining how something can be done

help key

(i) (on an Apple Macintosh) special key that displays help information; (ii) (on an IBM PC) F1 function key used to display help information

help screen

display of information about a program or function

Hercules graphics adapter (HGA)

standard for high-resolution mono graphics adapter developed by Hercules Corporation that can display text or graphics at a resolution of 720x348 pixels

Hertz (Hz)

SI unit of frequency, defined as the number of cycles per second of time; Hertz rate is the frequency at which mains electricity is supplied to the consumer. The Hertz rate in the USA and Canada is 60; in Europe it is 50

Hewlett Packard™

manufacturer of computers, test equipment, and printers

Hewlett Packard Graphics Language (HPGL)

page description language with a standard set of commands used to describe graphics

Hewlett Packard Interface Bus (HPIB)

standard method of interfacing peripheral devices or test equipment and computers

Hewlett Packard LaserJet *or* HP LaserJet

laser printer manufactured by Hewlett Packard that uses its PCL language to describe a page

Hewlett Packard Printer Control Language (HP-PCL)

page description language with a standard set of commands developed by Hewlett Packard to allow a software application to control functions of its LaserJet range of printers

hex *or* hexadecimal notation

number system using base 16 and digits 0-9 and A-F

HFS

HIERACHICAL FILING SYSTEM
(in an Apple Macintosh system) method used to store and organise files on a disk or CD-ROM
see also
HIGH SIERRA

HGA

HERCULES GRAPHICS ADAPTER

Hi-8

video cassette tape format that uses 8mm wide tape; mostly used in camcorders

hidden lines

lines which make up a three-dimensional object, but are obscured by a surface closer to the viewer when displayed as a two-dimensional image so are only seen when the three-dimensional object is viewed as a wire-frame model before it is rendered

hidden line algorithm
mathematical formula that removes hidden lines from a two-dimensional computer image of a 3-D object

hidden line removal
erasure of lines which should not be visible when looking at a two-dimensional image of a three-dimensional object

hierarchical filing system (HFS)
(in an Apple Macintosh system) method used to store and organise files on a disk or CD-ROM

hierachical vector quantization (HVQ)
video compession standard which allows colour video images to be transmitted in a bandwidth of 112Kbps

high definition television *or* HDTV
broadcast television standard that can display very clear images with much better definition than existing television sets; there are several standards: the Japanese standard, MUSE, uses 1125 lines/screen, the European standard, HD-MAC, uses 1250 lines/screen

high-end
expensive or high-performance device

high fidelity
refers to stereo sound recorded in 16 bits at a sample rate of 44.1KHz

high-level (programming) language (HLL)
computer programming language which is easy to learn and allows the user to write programs using words and commands that are easy to understand and look like English words; the program is then translated into machine code, with one HLL command often representing a number of machine code instructions

high memory
(on an IBM PC) memory area between 640Kb and 1Mb

high memory area (HMA)
(in an IBM PC) first 64Kb of extended memory above 1Mb that can be used by programs

high performance filing system (HPFS)
(in OS/2 operating system) method of storing file information that is faster and

more flexible than the basic OS/2 filing system or the MS-DOS FAT

high-resolution *or* hi-res
ability to display or detect a very large number of pixels per unit area; currently high-resolution graphics displays can show images at a resolution of 1024x1024 pixels, high-resolution printers can print at 600 or 800 dots per inch and a high-resolution scanner can scan at a resolution of 800 or 1200 dots per inch

High Sierra
early CD-ROM standard that then became the ISO 9660 standard (it was named after an area near Lake Tahoe, USA)

highlight
(i) to make characters or symbols stand out from the rest of the text, often by using bold type; (ii) property of an object that defines how it is displayed when a user selects it; for example, a button may flash or change colour when a user selects it; (iii) to select an object or text by dragging the pointer across it; when text is highlighted it normally appears inverted (white on a black background)

highlight bar
bar that a user can move up and down a list of options to choose an option

histogram
graph showing the density of the colour spectrum in an image

HLL
HIGH-LEVEL LANGUAGE

HMA
HIGH MEMORY AREA
(in an IBM PC) first 64Kb of extended memory above 1Mb that can be used by programs

HMI
HUMAN MACHINE INTERFACE
facilities provided to improve the interaction between a user and a computer system

HMS time format
system used by MCI to express time in hours, minutes and seconds - normally used only for videodisc devices

hologram

three-dimensional image produced by the interference pattern when part of a coherent light source, such as a laser, is reflected from an object and mixed with the main beam

home key

(on an PC) key that normally moves the cursor to the beginning of a line of text

horizontal blanking period

time taken for the picture beam in a monitor to return to the start of the next line from the end of the previous line

horizontal scan frequency

the number of lines on a video display that are refreshed each second; (a display with a resolution of 200 lines refreshed 60 times per second requires a horizontal scan frequency of 12KHz)
compare with
VERTICAL SCAN FREQUENCY

horizontal scrollbar

(in a GUI) bar along the bottom of a window which indicates that the page is wider than the window; a user can move horizontally across the page by dragging the indicator bar on the scrollbar

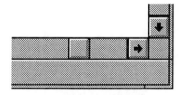

Horizontal scrollbar

horizontal scrolling

to move across a page, horizontally

horizontal wraparound

movement of a cursor on a computer display from the end of one line to the beginning of the next

hot key

action of pressing two or more keys at the same time to perform a function

hot link

command within a hypertext program that links a hotspot or hotword on one page with a second destination page which is displayed if the user selects the hotspot

hotspot
special area on an image or display that does something when the cursor is moved onto it or it is selected

hotword
word within displayed text that does something when the cursor is moved onto it or it is selected; often displayed in a different colour and used to define complex words or link one text to another

HP
HEWLETT PACKARD

HP-PCL
HEWLETT PACKARD PRINTER CONTROL LANGUAGE

HPFS
HIGH PERFORMANCE FILING SYSTEM
(in OS/2 operating system) method of storing file information that is faster and more flexible than the basic OS/2 filing system or the MS-DOS FAT

HPIB
HEWLETT PACKARD INTERFACE BUS

HPGL
HEWLETT PACKARD GRAPHICS LANGUAGE

HSV
HUE, SATURATION AND VALUE

HTML
HYPERTEXT MARKUP LANGUAGE
tagging codes used to define a hypertext document - normally used to define screens used in the World Wide Web on the Internet, similar to SGML; for example, the '<p>' code means new paragraph, the '<b>' code means display in bold
see also
SGML

hue
wavelength of a colour, used to describe the quality of a colour

hue, saturation and value (HSV)

method of defining a colour through its three properties: hue - the wavelength; saturation - the purity of the hue; and value - the brightness
see also
RGB, CMYK

Huffman encoding

data compression encoding method in which frequent characters are coded more efficiently and occupy less space than characters that appear less frequently in the data

huge model

(in programming) memory model of an Intel processor that allows data and program code to exceed 64Kb (but the total of both must be less than 1Mb)

human-computer *or* human-machine interface (HMI)

facilities provided to improve the interaction between a user and a computer system

HVQ

HIERARCHICAL VECTOR QUANTIZATION
video compession standard which allows colour video images to be transmitted in a bandwidth of 112Kbps

HyperCard™

multimedia authoring system in which a programmer can define cards which are separate pages with images, text, graphics, buttons, and other objects; jumps, links and effects are programmed using the HyperTalk programming language; used to produce hypertext documents; a title with a number of cards is called a stack; it was developed by Apple

hyperlink

series of commands attached to a button or word in one page that link it to another page in a multimedia book, so that if a user clicks on the button or word, the hyperlink will move the user to another position in the book or display another page

hypermedia

hypertext document that is also capable of displaying images and sound

HyperTalk™

scripting language used to define the elements in a HyperCard database, document or card

hypertext

system of organizing information; certain words in a document link to other documents or move the user to another position in the book, or display the text when the hotword is selected

hypertext markup language

see
HTML

hyphenation

splitting of a word (as at the end of a line, when the word is too long to fit)

hyphenation and justification (H & J)

justifying lines to a set width so that both left and right ends are level with the margins, and splitting long words correctly at the end of each line

Hz

HERTZ

I-beam

cursor shaped like the letter 'I' used (in a GUI) to edit text or indicate text operations

IBM™

INTERNATIONAL BUSINESS MACHINES

largest computer company in the world; developed the first PC based on the Intel processor

IBM AT

personal computer based on the Intel 80286 16-bit processor and featuring an ISA expansion bus

IBM AT keyboard

keyboard layout that features 12 function keys in a row along the top of the keyboard, with a separate numeric keypad

IBM-compatible

generic term for a personal computer that is hardware and software compatible with the IBM PC regardless of which Intel processor it uses; it features an ISA, EISA or MCA expansion bus

IBM PC

personal computer based on the Intel 8088 8-bit processor

129

IBM PC keyboard

keyboard layout that features 10 function keys arranged to the left of the main keys, with no separate numeric keypad

IBM PS/2 *or* IBM Personal System/2

range of personal computers based on the Intel 8086, 80286 and 80386 processors that feature an MCA expansion bus

IBM XT

personal computer based on the IBM PC but with an internal hard disk drive and featuring an ISA expansion bus

IC

INTEGRATED CIRCUIT

device consisting of a small piece of a crystal of a semiconductor onto which are etched or manufactured (by doping) a number of components such as transistors, resistors and capacitors, which together perform a function

icon

graphic symbol or small picture displayed on screen, used in an interactive computer system to provide an easy way of identifying a function; for example, the icon for a word-processor icon might be a small picture of a typewriter

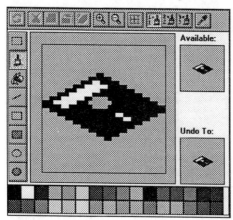

Icon design software for developers.

icon resource

file that contains the bitmap image of an icon, used by a programmer when writing an application

identifier *or* ID
set of characters used to distinguish between different resources in a multimedia book; each button, image, sound and text is given a unique identifier that allows a programmer to identify and control the object from a program script

IDE
INTEGRATED DRIVE ELECTRONICS
popular standard for hard disk drive unit that includes the control electronics on the drive; used in the Macintosh 630 series and in most PC-compatibles - this drive controller is cheaper than SCSI but cannot manage as high capacity drives as SCSI

identity palette
256 colour palette in which the first and last 10 colours are the system colours; used to speed up the process of loading bitmap files

IFF
INTERNATIONAL FILE FORMAT
(in CD-i) standard for compressed files stored on a CD-i

IFF
INTERCHANGE FILE FORMAT
standard that defines how palette data is stored in an Amiga and some graphics program

IH
see
INTERRUPT HANDLER

IMA
INTERNATIONAL MIDI ASSOCIATION
association that distributes information on the MIDI specification

IMA
INTERACTIVE MULTIMEDIA ASSOCIATION
professional organisation that covers subjects including authoring languages, formats, and intellectual property

image
(i) exact duplicate of an area of memory; (ii) copy of an original picture or design

image area

region of microfilm or display screen on which characters or designs can be displayed

image buffer

area of memory that is used to build up an image before it is transferred to screen

image compression

compressing the data that forms an image

image editing

altering or adjusting an image using a paint package or special image editing program; normally this means cropping, cutting and pasting, changing colours or retouching parts of an image

image enhancement

adjusting parts of an image using special image editing program, normally to change the contrast, brightness or sharpness of an image

image processing

analysis of information contained in an image, usually to enhance the image or to create special effects; for example, to adjust the colour balance, sharpen the image, etc.

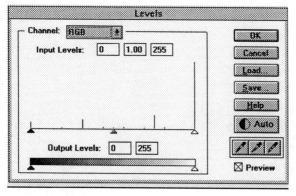

Image procesing applications allow a designer to adjust contrast, colour or brightness levels.

image processor

software that can be used for image processing, and to extract information from the image

image scanner
input device which converts documents or drawings or photographs into a digitized, machine-readable form

image setter
typesetting device that can process a PostScript page and produce a high-resolution output
see also
TYPESETTER

image stability
ability of a display screen to provide a flicker-free picture

image storage space
region of memory in which a digitized image is stored

image table
two bit-mapped tables used to control input and output devices or processes

imaging
process of creating an electronic representation of a picture by scanning

imaging system
equipment and software used to capture, digitize and compress video or still images

impact printer
printer that prints text and symbols by striking an ink ribbon onto paper with a metal character, such as a daisy-wheel printer (as opposed to a non-impact printer like a laser printer)

import
to convert a file stored in one format to a format that can be used by another program

indent
(i) space or series of spaces from the left margin, when starting a line of text;
(ii) to start a line of text with a space in from the left margin

index
(in a database) table of keywords that contains references to entries in the database; this index can be searched more rapidly than the entire database

index page

page of a multimedia book that lists all the other pages within the book and allows a user to locate other pages or areas of interest; normally provides buttons, hypertext or hotwords to the pages listed in the contents

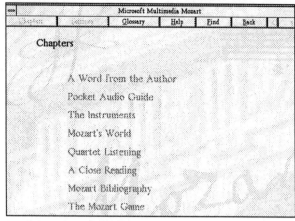

The index page of this multimedia application lists the main chapters together with control menu bar along the top of the screen.

Industry Standard Architecture

see
ISA

information provider (ip)

company or user who provides an information source for use in a videotext system or on the Internet (such as the company providing weather information or stock market reports)

infrared controller

remote control unit used to control a slide projector or camera

inherit

(in object-oriented programming) one class or data type that acquires the characteristics of another

inheritance

(in object-oriented programming) to pass the characteristics of one class or data type to another (called its descendant)

initialize

to set values or parameters or control lines to their initial values, to allow a program or process to be re-started

ink

(i) dark liquid used to mark or write with; (ii) colour selected that appears when you paint or draw using a drawing program on a computer

ink effect

features of Windows Movie Player utility that defines how cast members are drawn; for example, transparent ink effect displays the cast member with the background showing through

ink-jet printer

computer printer that produces characters by sending a stream of tiny drops of electrically charged ink onto the paper (the movement of the ink drops is controlled by an electric field; this is a non-impact printer with few moving parts)

input

to transfer data into a computer

input-bound *or* input-limited

(program) which is not running as fast as it could since it has to wait for data from a slower peripheral

input/output (I/O)

referring to receiving or transmitting data
see also
I/O

Ins *or* insert key

key that switches a word-processor or editor program into insert mode rather than overwrite mode

insert mode

mode of a wordprocessor or editing program in which characters are inserted into the text as a user types them in, rather than replacing existing characters

insertion point

cursor positioned to show where any text typed in will be entered within a document; usually shown by an I-beam cursor

install program

software utility that transfers program code from the distribution disks onto a computer's hard disk and configures the program

installable device driver
device driver that is loaded into memory and remains resident, replacing a similar function built into the operating system

instance
(i) one copy of an application, routine or object; for example, Microsoft Windows will let you run several copies of the same program at the same time, each is called an instance of the original; (ii) (in object-oriented programming) an object or duplicate object that has been created

instant jump
(in a videodisc player) hardware feature that allows the player to skip a number of frames (up to 200) in the time it takes to refresh the screen

instrument
electronic device that can produce a sound in response to a MIDI note or to a keyboard press

integer
mathematical term to describe a whole number (it may be positive or negative or zero)

integrated circuit (IC)
device consisting of a small piece of a crystal of a semiconductor onto which are etched or manufactured (by doping) a number of components such as transistors, resistors and capacitors, which together perform a function

integrated drive electronics
see
IDE

integrated services digital network
see
ISDN

Intel™
company which developed the first commercially available microprocessor (the 4004); they also developed the range of processors that are used in IBM PCs and compatible computers

Intel 8086
microprocessor that uses a 16-bit data bus and can address up to 1Mb of RAM

Intel 8088

microprocessor that uses a 16-bit data bus internally, but uses an 8-bit data bus externally; used in the first IBM PC computers

Intel 80286

microprocessor that uses a 16-bit data bus and can address up to 16Mb of RAM

Intel 80386

microprocessor that uses a 32-bit data bus and can address up to 4Gb of RAM

Intel 80486

microprocessor that uses a 32-bit data bus and can address up to 64Gb of RAM

Intel Pentium™

latest, most advanced microprocessor that has replaced the 80486 and uses a 32-bit data bus

interactive

(i) multimedia system in which a user can issue a command and the program responds or the user can control actions and control the way a program works; (ii) (system or piece of software) that allows communication between the user and the computer; (iii) display system that is able to react to different inputs from the user; (iv) computer mode that allows the user to enter commands or programs or data and receive immediate responses

interactive multimedia association (IMA)

professional organisation that covers subjects including authoring languages, formats, and intellectual property

interactive TV

channel that allows two-way communication between the viewer and broadcasting station; this feature often allows the user to choose which programme to watch or respond directly to questions displayed on-screen

interactive video *or* IV

system that uses a computer linked to a video disk player to provide processing power and real images or moving pictures; this system is often used in teaching to ask a student questions, which if answered correctly will provide him with a filmed sequence from the videodisk

interchange file format (IFF)
standard that defines how palette data is stored in an Amiga and some graphics programs

interface card
add-on board that allows a computer to interface to certain equipment or conform to a certain standard

interference
unwanted noise on a signal

interframe coding
system of compressing video images such that only the differences between each frame are recorded

interlace
method of building up an image on a television screen using two passes, each displaying alternate lines; this system uses two picture fields made up of alternate lines to reduce picture flicker effects

interlaced video
video signal made up of two separate fields - this is the normal display mode for home video

interleave factor
ratio of sectors skipped between access operations on a hard disk; in a hard disk with an interleave factor of 3, the first sector is read, then three sectors are skipped and the next sector is read. This is used to allow hard disks with slow access time to store more data on the disk

international file format (IFF)
(in CD-i) standard for compressed files stored on a CD-i

International MIDI Association (IMA)
professional organisation that covers subjects including authoring languages, formats, and intellectual property

Internet
international wide area network that provides file and data transfer, together with electronic mail functions for millions of users around the world; anyone can use the Internet and access any of the several million computers that are linked (by telephone)

see also
WWW

internet protocol (IP)

TCP/IP standard that defines how data is transferred across a network

internet protocol address (IP Address)

unique, 32-bit number which identifies each computer connected to a TCP/IP network

interoperability

the ability of two devices or computers to exchange information

interpreter

software used to translate (at the time of execution) a user's high-level program into machine code; a compiler translates the high-level language into machine code and then executes it, rather than the real-time translation by an interpreter
compare
COMPILER

interrupt

signal which diverts a central processing unit from one task to another which has higher priority, allowing the CPU to return to the first task later

interrupt-driven

(program) that works in response to an interrupt

interrupt handler (IH)

software that accepts interrupt signals and acts on them (such as running a special routine or sending data to a peripheral)

interrupt level

priority assigned to the interrupt from a peripheral

interrupt requests

see
IRQS

inverse video

video effect created by swapping the background and foreground display colours; so, for example, inverse text appears as black text on a white background instead of white text on a black background

invisible

guide or object visible on a DTP page or graphics layout during the design phase, but it not printed

I/O

INPUT/OUTPUT
referring to the receiving or transmitting of data

I/O address

the memory location that is used by an I/O port to transfer data with the CPU

I/O bound

processor that is doing very little processing since its time is taken up reading or writing data from a I/O port

I/O buffer

temporary storage area for data waiting to be input or output

I/O bus

links allowing data and control signal transfer between a CPU and memory or peripheral devices

I/O device

peripheral (such as a terminal in a workstation) which can be used for both inputting and outputting data to a processor

I/O mapping

method of assigning a special address to each I/O port that does not use any memory locations
compare
MEMORY MAPPING

I/O port

circuit or connector that provides an input/output channel to between a processor and another device
see also
SERIAL PORT, PARALLEL PORT

ion deposition

printing technology that works in a similar way to a laser printer, but instead of using light, it uses a printhead that deposits ions to create a charged image which attracts the toner; used for very high-speed printers

i/p *or* I/P
INPUT

ip
INFORMATION PROVIDER
company or user who provides an information source for use in a videotext system or on the Internet (such as a company providing weather information or stock market reports)

IP
INTERNET PROTOCOL
TCP/IP standard that defines how data is transferred over a network

IP address
unique, 32-bit number which identifies each computer connected to a TCP/IP network

ip terminal
special visual display unit that allows users to create and edit videotext pages before sending them to the main videotext page database

IRQs
INTERRUPT REQUESTS
hardware interrupts; an IRQ is a signal sent to the central processing unit (CPU) to temporarily suspend normal processing and transfer control to an interrupt handling routine.

IRQ	Device (in a PC)
0 -	System timer
1 -	Keyboard
2 -	Bus mouse or network card
3 -	COM2, COM4
4 -	COM1, COM3
5 -	LPT2, CD-ROM
6 -	Floppy disk
7 -	LPT1, sound card
8 -	Realtime clock
9 -	not used
10 -	not used
11 -	not used
12 -	not used
13 -	Maths coprocessor
14 -	Hard disk
15 -	not used

iris

small hole in a camera between the lens and the film; the iris is normally variable in size to adjust the amount of light passing through it to the film

ISA

INDUSTRY STANDARD ARCHITECTURE

standard used for the 16-bit expansion bus in an IBM PC or compatible; this has been replaced as a standard in more powerful PCs by either the MCA or EISA bus which provide a 32-bit data path and bus-mastering; local bus is often used for perhiperals that require high-speed data transfer, such as a network or graphics adapter; there are two types: the VL-bus (from VESA) and Intel's PCI bus - both allow direct data transfer between main memory and the peripheral

ISDN

INTEGRATED SERVICES DIGITAL NETWORK

standard method of transmitting digital data over a telephone network at high speeds - faster than a normal modem

ISO 9660

standard method of storing files on a CD-ROM, used in many formats including PhotoCD; its predecessor was High Sierra

isometric view

(in graphics) a drawing that shows all three dimensions of an object in equal proportion; an isometric view does not show any perspective

italic

character font in which the characters slope to the right

item

single thing among many; for example, one object in a multimedia book or one cell in a spreadsheet

IV

see
INTERACTIVE VIDEO

Jj

jack

plug which consists of a single pin; normally used with audio equipment (such as a headphone or microphone)

jaggies

jagged edges which appear along diagonal or curved lines displayed on a computer screen, caused by the size of each pixel
see also
ANTI-ALIASING

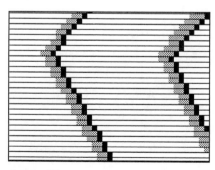

jaggies shown on diagonal lines

Jaguar™

multimedia console hardware developed by Atari, uses a 64-bit RISC processor and includes a high-speed graphics adapter and sound

jitter

fault where there is rapid small up-and-down movement of characters or pixels on a screen or image bits in a facsimile transmission

joint photographic expert group

see
JPEG

joystick

device that allows a user to move a cursor around the screen by moving an upright rod connected to an I/O port on the computer; mostly used for computer games or CAD or desktop publishing packages

joystick port

circuit and connector used to interface a joystick with a computer

JPEG™

JOINT PHOTOGRAPHIC EXPERTS GROUP
ISO/CCITT standard for compressing images that provides lossy compression; the compressed image is not as sharp as the original; JPEG can either work through hardware or software routines and works as follows: the image is divided into a matrix of tiny pixels, every other pixel is ignored and the grid is divided into blocks of 8x8 pixels, the algorithm then calculates the average of the blocks and so can delete one block - the decompression is the reverse of this process. MPEG is a similar standard that is used with full-motion colour digital video

JPEG++™

this is an extension to JPEG that allows parts of an image to be compressed differentially: for example, the background could be highly compressed (since it doesn't matter if this suffers a loss of quality)

jukebox

CD-ROM player that can hold several discs at the same time and load and play a disc automatically

jump

programming command to end one set of instructions and direct the processor to another section of the program

justify

to align text so that it is level on both right and left margins, normally by adding spaces between words

Kk

Kaleida Labs™
company formed as a joint venture between Apple and IBM to produce cross-platform multimedia authoring tools, the first of which is called ScriptX
see also
SCRIPTX

Kbit
KILOBIT
measure of 1,024 bits of data

KB *or* Kbyte
KILOBYTE
unit of measure for high capacity storage devices meaning 1,024 bytes; 1,024 is the strict definition in computer or electronics applications, being equal to a convenient power of two; these abbreviations can also be taken to equal approximately one thousand, even in computing applications. 1Kb is roughly equal to 1,000 output characters in a PC

kernel
basic essential instruction routines required as a basis for any operation in a computer system; (in an operating system) code that carries out the basic or

essential tasks. Kernel routines are usually hidden from the user; they are used by the operating system for tasks such as loading a program or displaying text on a screen

kern
to adjust the space between pairs of letters so that they are printed closer together

key frame
(i) single picture in an animation that describes the main actions in the sequence; (ii) in hypertext document, a page that gives the user a choice of destination; (iii) (in full motion video) a frame that is recorded in full rather than being compressed or differentially recorded

kilohertz (KHz)
frequency of one thousand cycles per second

kilobit *or* Kbit
1,024 bits of data

kilobyte *or* KB *or* Kbyte
unit of measure for high capacity storage devices meaning 1,024 bytes;

kiosk
small booth with a screen, means of user input and a computer, used to provide information for the general public

kludge
(i) temporary correction made to a badly written or constructed piece of software or to a keyboarding error; (ii) hardware which should be used for demonstration purposes only

Kodak PhotoCD
see
PHOTOCD

label
(i) word or other symbol used in a computer program to identify a routine or statement or variable; (ii) character(s) used to identify a variable or piece of data or a file

label field
an item of data in a record that contains a label

label record
record containing identification for a stored file

lag
time taken for an image to be no longer visible after it has been displayed on a CRT screen (this is caused by long persistence phosphor)

LAN *or* lan
LOCAL AREA NETWORK

network where various terminals and equipment are all within a short distance of one another (at a maximum distance of about 500m, for example in the same building), and can be interconnected by cables
compare
WAN

LAN server
computer which runs a network operating system and controls the basic network operations; all the workstations in a LAN are connected to the central network server, and users log onto the network server

LAN Server™

IBM software product that controls access to a network server, manages file and printer sharing

landscape

orientation of a page or piece of paper where the longest edge is horizontal
compare
PORTRAIT

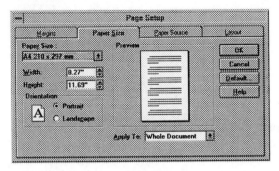

Landscape format is one option when printing a page, the other option is portrait format.

language

system of words and symbols which allows communication with computers (such as one that allows computer instructions to be entered as words which are easy for the user to understand and then translates them into machine code, which the computer can execute)

laptop computer

computer that is light enough to carry but not so small as to fit in a pocket; usually with a screen, keyboard and disk drive

large model

(in an Intel processor) memory model in which both code and data can exceed 64Kb in size, but combined size should be less than 1Mb; often used when programming graphics applications in C or C++

laser

LIGHT AMPLIFICATION BY STIMULATED EMISSION OF RADIATION
electical device that produces coherent light of a single wavelength in a narrow beam, used to read data from a CD-ROM and to charge points in a laser printer

LaserDisc

optical disc that is either 12, 20 or 30cm in diameter, used to store analog video and digital sound and generally used to refer to videodiscs that use the Philips LaserVision system

laser disc
see
COMPACT DISC

laser emulsion storage
digital storage technique using a laser to expose light-sensitive material

laser printer
high-resolution computer page printer that uses a laser source to print high-quality dot matrix character patterns on paper; it creates an image on a charged drum (using a laser), this then attracts particles of fine black toner, the drum transfers the image to the paper which is then heated to melt the toner onto the paper; a laser printer offers high-resolution printing with, typically, either 300 or 600dpi. NOTE: there are actually very few printers that use a laser, most use a laser diode or an LED light source for the same effect

LaserJet™ *or* Hewlett Packard LaserJet *or* HP LaserJet
laser printer manufactured by Hewlett Packard that uses its PCL language to describe a page (or PostScript in the newer LaserJet 4M series)

LaserVision™
original interactive videodisc format, developed by Philips, that provides analog video and two analog audio signals on a 30cm diameter disc; two formats are used to store the video images: CAV and CLV
see
CAV, CLV, VIDEODISC

LaserWriter™
laser printer, manufactured by Apple, primarily for use with Macintosh computers, that uses the PostScript page description language

latency
time delay between a user selecting a button or option and the software responding, often caused by having to load data from disk

launch
to start or run a program

layer
feature of graphics software that provides a stack of separate drawing areas

that can be overlayed to produce the final image, or controlled and manipulated independently; often used in complex images: for example, the background might be on layer 1, an image of a house on layer 2 and any special effects on layer 3 - the finished picture is made up of the three layers combined and viewed together

LCD

LIQUID CRYSTAL DISPLAY

liquid crystal that turns black when a voltage is applied, used in many watches, calculators and other small digital displays NOTE: there are several types of LCD display: Passive Matrix in which the transistors controlling the LCD pixels are outside of the display (provides sharp monochrome but a less defined colour image). To confuse the issue, there are two types of Passive Matrix: TN (twisted nematic) is used in cheaper screens and provides black on a grey background; STN (supertwisted nematic) is used on most laptops for both mono and colour displays. Active Addressing provides a sharper display than an equivalent Passive Matrix display. Dual Scan Passive Matrix effectively doubles the refresh rate of the screen and improves the sharpness of Passive Matrix colour screens. Active Matrix or thin film transistor LCD (TFT) is used in most high-end colour laptop screens; the controlling transistors are built into each pixel for each colour - this provides the best quality colour and contrast, but is the most expensive.

LCD shutter printer

page printer that uses an LCD panel in front of a bright light to describe images onto the photosensitive drum; the LCD panel stops the light passing through, except at pixels that describe the image - similar in operation and resolution to a laser printer, but has fewer moving parts

leading

space between lines of text, normally measured in points

learning curve

graphical description of how someone can acquire knowledge (about a product) over time; for example, a product with a steep learning curve is initally very difficult to use

LED

LIGHT EMITTING DIODE

semiconductor diode that emits light when a current is applied

LED printer

page printer (similar to a laser printer) that uses an LED light source instead of

a laser
see also
LASER PRINTER

left justify

printing command that makes the left hand margin of the text even; the right hand margin is ragged

letter-quality (LQ) printing

feature of some dot-matrix printers which prints out characters of the same quality as a typewriter by using a dot-matrix head that can produce very small dots which are very close together

Level A

ADPCM audio quality level with a 20KHz bandwidth, 38.7KHz sample rate and 8-bit samples

Level B

ADPCM audio quality level with a 17KHz bandwidth, 38.7KHz sample rate and 4-bit samples

Level C

ADPCM audio quality level with an 8.5KHz bandwidth, 18.9KHz sample rate and 4-bit samples

LF

LINE FEED

library

(i) software routine that a user can insert into his program to provide a function with no effort; (ii) a number of specially written or relevant software routines, which a user can insert into his own program, saving time and effort; (iii) a group of functions which a computer needs to refer to often, but which are not stored in main memory

library routine

prewritten routine that can be inserted into a main program and called up when required

light emitting diode

see
LED

light pen

computer accessory in the shape of a pen which contains a light-sensitive device that can detect pixels on a video screen (often used with suitable software to draw graphics on a screen or position a cursor)

LIM EMS

LOTUS, INTEL, MICROSOFT EXPANDED MEMORY SYSTEM

(in an IBM PC) standard that defines extra memory added above the 640Kb limit of conventional memory; this memory can only be used by specially-written programs

limits

pre-defined maximum ranges for numbers in a computer

limiter

device that removes any part of an input signal that is greater than or less than pre-defined limits; used with audio and video signals to prevent overloading an amplifier

line

(i) one trace by the electron picture beam on a screen or monitor; (ii) row of characters (printed on a page or displayed on a computer screen or printer)

line feed (LF)

control code on a printer or computer that moves the cursor down by one line

line flyback

electron beam returning from the end of one line to the beginning of the next

line frequency

number of picture lines that are scanned per second

line drawing

illustration in which objects are drawn using thin lines, without shading or surface texture
see also
WIREFRAME

linear search

search method which compares each item in a list with the search key until the correct entry is found (starting with the first item and working sequentially towards the end)

linear video

(i) continuous playback of a video sequence from videotape; (ii) normal video that is played back in a continuous sequence rather than a single frame at a time as in interactive video

linear video editing

video sequence (on videotape) that is edited by inserting or deleting new frames but without changing the order of the frames
see also
EDL

linearity

the shape of the frequency response curve of a device (such as a microphone or A/D converter); if the curve is straight, the device is very accurate, if it is not, the device is introducing frequency distrortion

line spacing

space between lines of text; this is often described as a multiple of the leading plus the size of the type, for example single or double line space
see also
LEADING

line style

appearance of a line displayed on screen or printed; for example, the line could be made up of dashes or solid

Lingo™

scripting language used to control the actions in the Macromedia Director authoring software

link

(i) to combine separate routines from different files and library files to create a program; (ii) (in hypertext) to create an association between two objects in a title, for example to link a button to another page in the title that is displayed when the user selects the button

linked list

list of data where each entry carries the address of the next consecutive entry

linked subroutine

number of computer instructions in a program that can be called at any time, with control being returned on completion to the next instruction in the main program

linked object

(in Windows) feature of OLE that allows one object or document or image to be referenced and displayed in another document; only a link is inserted and the originating application must be present
compare with
EMBEDDED OBJECT

liquid crystal display

see
LCD

list

data elements separated by commas

list box

display element in GUIs that can show a list of items (such as files in a directory) and allows a user to move a bar up and down the list to choose an item; the list box is normally intelligent enough to add a scroll bar if there are more items that can fit in the box

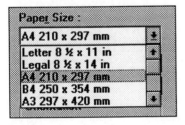

List box displays a scrolling list of options within a single option.

LIST chunk

(in a RIFF file) four-character code LIST that contains a series of subchunks

LLL

LOW-LEVEL LANGUAGE
programming language similar to assembler, in which each instruction has a single equivalent machine code instruction (the language is particular to one system or computer)
see also
HLL

local area network *or* LAN

network where various terminals and equipment are all a short distance from one another (at a maximum distance of about 500m, for example in the same

building) and can be interconnected by cables
compare
WAN

local bus
direct link or bus between a device and the processor, with no logic circuits or buffers or decoders in between

local declaration
assignment of a variable that is only valid in one section of a computer program or structure

local variable
variable which can only be accessed by certain routines in a certain section of a computer program
compare with
GLOBAL, SYSTEM VARIABLE

LocalTalk™
cabling system and connectors used in Apple's AppleTalk network

lock a file
to prevent any further writing to a file; often used in multi-user database applications to prevent someone writing changes to a file when another user is reading the data

lock onto
to synchronize an internal clock with a received signal

logical palette
(in Windows) graphics object that includes the colour palette information it requires; the application asks Windows if it can use these colours (in a process called realizing the palette)

LOGO
high-level programming language used mainly for educational purposes, with graphical commands that are easy to use

logo
set of characters or symbol used to identify a company or product

longitudinal time code (LTC)
method of recording a time code signal on a linear audio track along a video

tape; the disadvantage of this method is that the code is not readable at slow speeds or when the tape has stopped
compare with
VITC

look-up table *or* LUT

collection of stored results that can be accessed very rapidly by a program without the need to calculate each result whenever needed; normally used to store colour, palette or image transform data

loop

procedure or series of instructions in a computer program that are performed again and again until a test shows that a specific condition has been met or until the program has been completed

lossless compression

image compression techniques that can reduce the number of bits used for each pixel in an image, without losing any information or sharpness (such as Huffman Encoding)

lossy compression

image compression techniques that can reduce the number of bits used for each pixel in an image, but in doing so loses information (such as JPEG)

Lotus™

software company best known for its desktop applications such as the spreadsheet program, 1-2-3 and networking products such as cc:Mail and Notes

loudspeaker

electromagnetic device that converts electrical signals into audible noise

low end

hardware or software that is not very powerful or sophisticated and is designed for beginners

low-level language (LLL)

programming language similar to assembler, in which each instruction has a single equivalent machine code instruction (the language is particular to one system or computer)
see also
HIGH-LEVEL LANGUAGE

low memory
(in a PC) memory locations up to 640Kb
compare
HIGH MEMORY

lower case
small characters (such as a, b, c, as opposed to upper case A, B, C)

LTC
see
LONGITUDINAL TIME CODE

luminance
part of a video signal or image that defines the brightness at each point
see also
YUV

LUT
see
LOOK-UP TABLE

LV
see
LASERVISION

LV-ROM
12-inch diameter optical disc developed by Philips that can store both analog video and digital data

Mm

M
MEGA
(i) one million; (ii) in computing this means 1,048,576 (equal to 2^{20})

mA
MILLIAMPERE
electrical current measure equal to one thousandth of an ampere

Mac
see
MACINTOSH

MacBinary™
file storage and transfer system that allows Macintosh files, together with their icons and long file names, to be stored on other computer systems

Macintosh™
range of personal computers designed by Apple Corporation; the Macintosh used the Motorola family of processors, the 68000, while the newest models now use the PowerPC RISC processor; the Macintosh is best known for its graphical user interface which allows a user to control the computer with icons and a mouse.

macro
series of commands or program routine or block of instructions identified by a single word

Macromedia Director™
authoring software for the PC and Macintosh using the Lingo scripting language

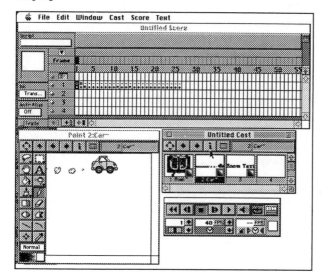

Macromedia Director is uses a score (top) that displays the actions of the cast (middle, right)

magazine
number of pages in a multimedia book or videotext system

magnetic recording
transferring an electrical signal onto a moving magnetic tape or disk by means of a magnetic field generated by a write head

magneto-optical recording
high-capacity storage media that uses an optical disc; the optical disk has a thin layer of magnetic film which is heated by a laser, the particles are then polarised by a weak magnetic field. Magneto-optical media has a very high capacity (over 600Mb) and is re-writable

magnitude
level or strength of a signal or variable

main body (of a program)
set of instructions that form the main part of a program and from which other subroutines are called

main clock
clock signal that synchronizes all the components in a system

male connector
plug with conducting pins that can be inserted into a female connector to provide an electrical connection

Mandlebrot set
mathematical equation that is called recursively to generate a set of values; when plotted these form a fractal image
see also
FRACTAL

manipulate
to move, edit and change text or data

man machine interface (MMI)
hardware and software designed to make it easier for users to communicate effectively with a machine

manual
document containing instructions about the operation of a system or piece of software

map
(i) diagram representing the internal layout of a computer's memory or communications regions; (ii) data that is linked to another set of data; (iii) list of data items or objects within an application or multimedia book; (iv) to transfer data from one region of memory to another; for example, a graphic image is mapped in main memory and on the display; (v) to relate or link one set of data items with another
see also
BIT-MAP

margin
blank space around a section of text

marquee
(in a graphics application) area selected by a selection tool

mask
to select areas of an image that are not to be transformed by subsequent special effects or paint operations; for example, an image of a man in a field

could be masked out and the background blurred to make him stand out more as a sharp image on a blurred background

master disc
glass disc onto which a laser etches pits to represent data - the glass disc is then used to press the plastic discs ready for distribution

mastering
process to convert finished data to a master disc

mat
plain coloured border that is displayed around an image that is smaller than the window in which it is displayed

matte
(in video or film) specified region within an image which can be coded to appear transparent or opaque - used to reveal or mask off part of an image in another plane; normally used for special effects in which an object is photographed against a (normally blue) background which is then replaced with another image to give the impression that the object appears against that image
see also
CHROMA KEY

maximise
(in MS-Windows) to expand an application icon back to its original display window; you maximise a window by clicking once on the up arrow in the top right hand corner
compare
MINIMISE

Mb
MEGABIT
equal to 1,048,576 bits of storage, or equal to 131,072 bytes

MB *or* MByte
MEGABYTE
equal to 1,048,576 bytes of storage, or equal to 2^{20} bytes

MCA
MICROCHANNEL ARCHITECTURE™
design of the expansion bus within IBM's PS/2 range of personal computers that has taken over from the older ISA/AT bus; MCA is a 32-bit bus that

supports bus master devices

MCGA
MULTICOLOR GRAPHICS ADAPTER
colour graphics adapter standard fitted in low-end IBM PS/2 computers
> APPENDIX: PC GRAPHICS

MCI
MEDIA CONTROL INTERFACE
device-independent programming interface, developed by IBM and Microsoft,
that provides basic control (such as play, stop, rewind) of installed multimedia
devices from within a programming language such as C and Visual Basic; MCI
is part of Microsoft Windows 3.1 - the Windows Media Player is a simple front-
end that issues MCI commands to any installed multimedia device (such as to
play a CD audio disc, video clip or sound file)

MCI device
recognised multimedia device that is installed in a computer with the correct
drivers; for example, a sound card could either be installed with an MCI driver
or with its own proprietary driver

MDA
MONOCHROME DISPLAY ADAPTER
video adapter standard used in early PC systems that could display text in 25
lines of 80 columns
> APPENDIX: PC GRAPHICS

MDK
MULTIMEDIA DEVELOPER'S KIT
product developed by Microsoft that allows developers to produce multimedia
applications more easily using the supplied libraries of routines to control video
playback, process images and display text

mechanical mouse
pointing device that is operated by moving it across a flat surface; as the
mouse is moved, a ball inside spins and turns two sensors that feed the
horizontal and vertical movement back to the computer
compare
OPTICAL MOUSE

media control interface
see
MCI

162

Media Player™

utility supplied with Microsoft Windows 3.1 that allows the user to control installed multimedia hardware and pass data to the device - such as playing an audio CD-ROM, a video clip or a sound file through a sound card; the Media Player utility is actually a simple front-end that issues MCI commands to a multimedia device

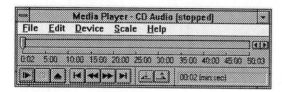

Media Player utility.

media server

file server on a local area network that is primarily used to store multimedia data (such as sound, images, and video)

medium

method used to communicate with an end-user, e.g. film, sound, or text

medium model

memory model of the Intel 80x86 processor family that allows 64Kb of data and up to 1MB of code; used when writing applications in assembly anguage, C or C++

meg

MEGABYTE

mega- (M)

(i) meaning one million; (ii) meaning 1,048,576 (equal to 2^{20}) and used only in computing and electronic related applications

MegaCD™

add-on to a console games system with a built-in CD-ROM drive to play interactive titles; developed by Sega, the MegaCD plugs into a Mega-Drive console

megabit (Mb)

equal to 1,048,576 bits, or equal to 131,072 bytes

megabyte (MB)

equal to 1,048,576 bytes of storage, or equal to 2^{20} bytes

163

Mega-Drive™
interactive console that can run titles from cartridge or CD; developed by Sega

megahertz (MHz)
measure of frequency equal to one million cycles per second

megapixel display
display adapter and monitor that are capable of displaying over one million pixels; this means a resolution of at least 1,024x1,024 pixels

Mega VGA
256 colour Super VGA mode with a resolution of 1024x768 that requires one megabyte of video RAM

melody
series of musical notes that form the basis for a musical tune

member
(i) one object on a page of a multimedia book; (ii) individual record or item in a field

memo field
field in an application that allows a user to add comments or a memo about the entry; memo fields cannot normally be searched but can store a larger amount of text than a normal text field

memory map
diagram indicating the allocation of address ranges to various devices such as RAM, ROM and memory-mapped input/output devices

memory-mapped
(i) I/O device that is allocated an address to allow it to be accessed as if it was a memory location; (ii) screen in which each pixel is allocated a memory address so that images are displayed by changing the contents of the memory address

memory model
method used in a program to address the code and data that are used within that program; the memory model defines how much memory is available for code and data; processors with a segmented address space (like the Intel 80x86 range) can support multiple memory models

memory page

one section of main store which is divided into pages, and which contains data or programs

menu

list of options or programs available to the user; a pop-up menu is normally displayed in the centre of the screen; a pull-down menu is displayed below the relevant entry on a menu-bar

menu-bar

(in a GUI) list of options available to a user which are displayed on a horizontal line along the top of the screen or window: each menu option activates a pull-down menu

menu-driven software

program where commands or options are selected from a menu by the operator rather than commands typed in by the user at a prompt

menu item

one of the choices in a menu

menu selection

choosing commands from a list of options presented to the operator

message

(i) (in an object-oriented programming system) code generated by an action or object and interpreted by another object; for example, if a user presses the mouse button it generates a 'button_down' message that can then be interpreted by a user-interface or program; (ii) text displayed to a user to report on a condition or program; (iii) (in MIDI) data that is sent to control an instrument

message box

small window displayed on screen with text that informs the user of a condition, error or report

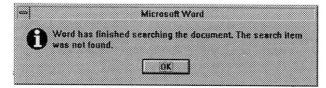

Message Box

metafile

(i) file that contains other files; (ii) file that defines or contains data about other files

MFM

MODIFIED FREQUENCY MODULATION

method of storing data on magnetic media (such as a magnetic disk) that encodes the data bit according to the state of the previous bit; MFM is more efficient than FM, but less efficient than RLL encoding

MHz

MEGAHERTZ

measure of frequency equal to one million cycles per second

Micro Channel Architecture™ (MCA)

design of the expansion bus within IBM's PS/2 range of personal computers that has taken over from the older ISA/AT bus; MCA is a 32-bit bus that supports bus master devices

Micro Channel Bus™

proprietary 32-bit expansion bus defined by IBM in its Micro Channel Architecture

microphone

device that converts changes in air pressure (due to sound waves) into an electrical signal; you speak into a microphone and it produces a signal that represents the sound pressure

Microsoft™

the biggest developer and publisher of software for the PC and Macintosh; Microsoft developed the MS-DOS operating system for the IBM PC and later Windows, together with a range of application software

Microsoft Compact Disc Extensions

see
MSCDEX

Microsoft DOS (MS-DOS)™

operating system for IBM PC range of personal computers that manages data storage onto disks, display output and user input; MS-DOS is a single-user, single-tasking operating system that is controlled by a command-line interface in which a user types in commands rather than a mouse

Microsoft Windows 3.1™

multi-tasking graphical user interface designed to be easy to use; Windows uses icons to represent files and devices and can be controlled using a mouse, unlike MS-DOS which requires commands to be typed in

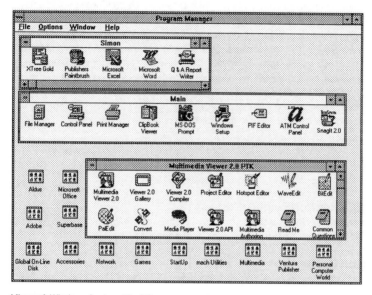

Microsoft Windows front-end for PCs.

Microsoft Windows 95™

multi-tasking graphical user interface that has superseded Windows 3.1; it provides full 32-bit software support and pre-emptive multitasking together with built-in networking and Internet support

Microsoft Windows for Workgroups™

multi-tasking GUI designed to be easy to use, that is compatible and nearly identical to Windows 3.1 but includes built-in networking support

MID-F1

(in CD-i) mid-quality sound at Level B
see
LEVEL B

MIDI

MUSICAL INSTRUMENT DIGITAL INTERFACE

serial interface - running at 32.5Kbps - that connects electronic instruments; the MIDI interface can connect up to 32 different instruments and carries signals from a sequencer or computer that instructs the different instruments - such as a drum machine or synthesizer - to play notes together with instructions called control-change messages, which control the volume, pitch and type of instrument used; NOTE: a MIDI interface does not carry sounds, rather it carries notes and instructions to change to a different preset sound; many PC sound cards include electronics to generate sounds from MIDI data on-board. There are two kinds of MIDI sound generation: FM synthesis simulates musical notes by modulating the frequency of a base carrier wave, whereas waveform synthesis uses digitized samples of the notes to produce a more realistic sound. MIDI also allows multiple different voices, or notes, to be played back simultaneously (MPC requires an 8-voice synthesizer, but studio-quality instruments can have up to 32 MIDI voices)

MIDI connector

standard 5-pin, round DIN connector used to connect MIDI devices

MIDI control-change message

message sent to a synthesizer to control the volume or pitch of a sound or to change the instrument patch used to generate a sound

MIDI device

device that can receive or send MIDI data

MIDI file

file format used to store a MIDI song, made up of notes and control-change messages (normally has a MID file extension)

MIDI interface card

adapter card that plugs into an expansion connector in a PC and allows it to send and receive MIDI data

MIDI Mapper

utility provided with Microsoft Windows that allows a user to redefine the way MIDI channels are used - for example, it can be used to send any data marked for channel two to channel four and also modify its controls, such as the volume setting

MIDI mapping

translating and redirecting MIDI messages between channels according to settings in a MIDI map

MIDI program-change message

message sent to a synthesizer to request a patch change for a particular MIDI channel

MIDI sequence

data that has time-sequence data embedded and that can be played by a MIDI sequencer

MIDI sequencer

(i) software that allows a user to record, edit, add special effects and playback MIDI data through a synthesizer; (ii) hardware device that records or plays back stored MIDI data

MIDI setup map

(used with MIDI Mapper) file that contains all the data required to define the settings for MIDI Mapper

MIDI time code (MTC)

messages used to synchronize MIDI sequences with an external device, such as an SMPTE time code

milliampere (mA)

measure of electrical current, equal to one-thousandth of an amp

millisecond (ms)

measure of time, equal to one-thousandth of a second

minimise

(in Microsoft Windows) to shrink an application window down to an icon, normally using the down-arrow button in the top-right-hand corner of the main window

MMA

MIDI MANUFACTURERS ASSOCIATION

MME

MULTIMEDIA EXTENSIONS

MMI

MAN MACHINE INTERFACE

hardware and software designed to make it easier for users to communicate effectively with a machine

mnemonic keyboard shortcut

shortcut to a menu option or function by pressing a special key sequence; normally this is a combination of the Alt key on a PC or the Apple key on a Mac at the same time as another key; the convention is that the second key is underlined. For example, the standard shortcut to pull-down the File menu in Windows is Alt-F (the F in File is underlined to show that it is the shortcut key)

modal

method of displaying a window so that the user cannot do anything outside this window; dialog boxes are normally modal windows and will not let you do anything outside the window until you choose an option or close the dialog box

Mode 1

encoding format used on compact discs, that has error-detection and correction codes, and is used in CD-ROM, DV-I and CD-TV - supports a data area of 2048bytes per sector

Mode 2

encoding format with two forms: form 1 is the same as Mode 1, form 2 requires no processing and the data can be sent straight to the output channel - this is used in CD-ROM XA, PhotoCD and CD-i. Mode 2 form 2 has a larger data area than Mode 1, since there is less error correction code

modelling

colouring and shading a (normally wire-frame or vecto) graphic object so that it looks solid and real

modified frequency modulation

MFM

Modula-2

high-level programming language derived from Pascal, that supports modular programming techniques and data abstraction

modulate

to change a carrier wave so that it can carry data

modulated signal

constant frequency and amplitude carrier signal that is used in a modulated form to transmit data

modulating signal

signal to be transmitted that is used to modulate a carrier

modulator

electronic circuit that varies a carrier signal according to an applied signal; often used to convert the output of a computer to a composite signal (by varying a generated carrier signal) that can be displayed on a standard television set

moire effect

interference pattern caused by the wrong screen angle being used for a particular printer
see
SCREEN ANGLE

monitor

(i) visual display unit used to display high quality text or graphics, generated by a computer, video camera or video recorder; monitors can be colour or monochrome and can display different resolution graphics depending on the dot pitch and refresh rate; (ii) software that displays the status or progress of an activity
see also
ANALOG MONITOR, DIGITAL MONITOR, MULTI-SCAN MONITOR

monochrome

(image) in one colour, usually shades of grey and black and white

monochrome display adapter (MDA)

video adapter standard used in early PC systems that could display text in 25 lines of 80 columns
>APPENDIX: PC GRAPHICS

monochrome monitor

computer monitor that displays text and graphics in black, white and shades of grey instead of colours

monophonic

sound recorded or played back through a single channel
compare with
STEREOPHONIC

monospacing

typeface or system of typesetting in which each character takes up the same amount of space
compare with
PROPORTIONAL

171

morphing

process of transforming one image into another over a period of time; usually used for special effects, for example to transform an image of a house into a bird in 20 separate frames so that the change appears animated when played back

montage

combining several still or video images

mosaic

(used in videotext systems) display character that is made up of small dots

motherboard

main printed circuit board of a system, containing the processor and most of the components and connections for expansion boards, etc.

Motorola™

manufacturer of electronic components, including the 68000 range of processors used in Apple Macintosh computers; its latest processor is the PowerPC - a RISC processor used in the current high-end range of Macintosh computers

Motorola 68000™

processor that can manage 32-bit words internally, but transfers data externally via a 16-bit data bus; used in the Apple Macintosh SE and Macintosh Plus

Motorola 68020™

processor similar to the 68000 that uses full internal and external 32-bit architecture

Motorola 68030™

processor similar to the 68020, that can manage 32-bit words internally and externally, but can run at much faster clock rates than the 68020

Motorola PowerPC™

RISC-based 32-bit processor used in high-end Macintosh computers and other high-performance workstations; it is still downwards compatible with the 68000 range

motion blur

blurring of an object that moves too fast to be frozen by the camera

motion control

computer that allows a user to control all the aspects of a camera to allow special effects in video or still images

motion picture experts group

see
MPEG

mouse

small hand-held input device moved on a flat surface to control the position of a cursor on the screen
see also
MECHANICAL, OPTICAL MOUSE

mouse-driven

(software) application which uses a mouse rather than a keyboard to control its actions

mouse driver

small, normally resident, driver program which converts positional data sent from a mouse to a standard form of coordinates that can be used by any software

mouse pointer

small arrow displayed on screen that moves around as the mouse is moved to indicate where the user is pointing on screen

movie file

data file used by Windows Movie Player that has an .MMM extension, the file contains graphic objects (the cast members) together with information that defines how they move around the screen

movie ID

unique ID number assigned to a movie in Movie Player - each separate instance has a different ID number

Movie Player™

Windows utility that can playback AVI-format video clips or movie files with the MMM extension

Movie Player instance

one copy of the Movie Player program that is running

MPC

MULTIMEDIA PC

minimum hardware requirements for a multimedia PC specified by the Multimedia PC Marketing Council; this gives the user a guide when buying a PC that is capable of running multimedia applications

MINIMUM REQUIREMENTS

	Level 1	Level 2
RAM	2MB	4MB
Processor	386SX 16MHz	486SX 25MHz
Floppy disk	1.44MB 3.5″	1.44MB 3.5″
Hard disk	30MB	160MB
CD-ROM	150KB transfer rate, 1 second access time	300KB transfer rate, 400 ms access time CD-ROM XA ready multisession
Sound	8-bit, 8 voice synthesizer MIDI playback	16-bit, 8 voice synthesizer MIDI playback
Video	640x480x16	640x480x64K
Ports	MIDI, joystick	MIDI, joystick

RECOMMENDED FEATURES

	Level 1	Level 2
RAM	—	8MB
CD-ROM	64KB on-board buffer	64KB on-board buffer
Sound	—	CD-ROM XA audio, support for IMA adopted ADPCM algorithm
Video	640x480x256	Able to deliver 1.2 megapixels per second without using more than 40% of CPU bandwidth

MPEG

MOTION PICTURE EXPERTS GROUP

full-motion video compression technique that is more efficient than the similar still-image compression scheme, JPEG; MPEG compares two successive frames and only records the changes between the two; MPEG-1 is used for data rates of 2Mb per second, MPEG-2 for data rates of 2-10Mb per second

ms
MILLISECOND
one thousandth of a second

MSCDEX
MICROSOFT COMPACT DISC ENTENSIONS
driver software installed on a PC to allow DOS and Windows to access a CD-ROM drive as a normal disk drive letter; normally drive D:

MS-DOS™
MICROSOFT DOS
operating system for IBM PC range of personal computers that manages data storage onto disks, display output and user input; MS-DOS is a single-user, single-tasking operating system that is controlled by a command-line interface

MSF time format
time format that counts frames per second used by MCI, normally used by CD-audio devices (in a CD-A device there are 75 frames per second)

MSX
hardware and software standard for home computers that can use interchangeable software

MTC
MIDI TIME CODE
messages used to synchronize MIDI sequences with an external device, such as an SMPTE time code

multicolour graphics adapter (MCGA)
colour graphics adapter standard fitted in low-end IBM PS/2 computers
> APPENDIX: PC GRAPHICS

MultiFinder™
version of Apple Macintosh Finder that supports multitasking

multi-frequency or multi-scan or multi-sync monitor
monitor that can accept video signals with different horizontal or vertical synchronizing frequencies and adjust to display the image; for example, a multi-frequency monitor can display VGA and SVGA resolutions which are at different frequencies

multimedia

the combination of sound, graphics, animation, video and text within an application

multimedia developer's kit (MDK)

product developed by Microsoft that allows developers to produce multimedia applications more easily using the supplied libraries of routines to control video playback, process images and display text

multimedia extensions (MME)

part of Microsoft Windows 3.1 that supports multimedia functions, specifically audio recording and playback, animation playback, MIDI, and MCI devices such as for CD-ROM and video players

multimedia PC

computer that can run multimedia application; normally equipped with a sound card, CD-ROM drive and high-resolution colour monitor
see also
MPC

multimedia ready

computer that has the necessary extra hardware to allow it to run multimedia applications; this normally means a PC or Macintosh that has a CD-ROM drive, sound card and graphics adapter, or that conforms to the MPC specification

multi-platform

software that can run on several different hardware platforms

multiscan monitor

see
MULTIFREQUENCY

multisession

CD-ROM which has had data stored onto it at different times (each time is called a session); this normally applies to PhotoCD discs - if the PhotoCD is not full, you can add extra images to it: this is a multisession disc because it contains images added after the first session

multisession compatible

drive that can read multisession discs; if you want to access a PhotoCD disc, you normally require a multisession compatible drive

multisync monitor
see
MULTIFREQUENCY

multitasking *or* multi-tasking
ability of a computer system to run two or more programs at the same time; few small systems are capable of simultaneous multitasking, since each program would require its own processor; this is overcome by allocating to each program an amount of processing time, executing each a little at a time so that they will appear to run simultaneously due to the speed of the processor and the relatively short gaps between programs; Microsoft Windows, IBM OS/2 and Apple System 7.5 are operating systems that are capable of multitasking several programs at the same time

multithreading
to run several different processes in rapid sucession within a program (effectively multitasking within a program)

music chip
integrated circuit capable of generating musical sounds and tunes

musical instrument digital interface
see
MIDI

Nn

name
a convenient identifier for an object that can be used to refer to the object from a script or command

nano- *or* n
meaning one thousand millionth or (in USA) one billionth

nanosecond *or* ns
one thousand millionth of a second

narrative
text or story that describes a video or animation

National Television Standards Committee (NTSC)
standard for television transmission and reception using a 525-line picture refreshed at 30 frames per second; the picture is broadcast using amplitude modulation and the sound using frequency modulation; NTSC is the standard in the USA, Central America and Japan. Most of Europe uses the PAL standard, except France which uses SECAM

navigation
moving around a multimedia title using hotspots, buttons and a user interface

needle
tiny metal pin on a dot matrix printer which prints one of the dots

network

series of computers, printers and peripherals linked together so that the resources and files can be shared by users

Newton™

range of PDAs developed by Apple

Nintendo™

major video game developer producing both software and hardware consoles

no-drop image

(in a GUI) icon image displayed during a drag and drop operation when the pointer is over an object that cannot be the destination object (the object being dragged cannot be dropped onto it)

node

connection point in a network

noise

random signal present in addition to any wanted signal, caused by static, temperature, power supply, magnetic or electric fields and also by stars and the sun

noise immunity

ability of a device or circuit to filter out or be protected from noise

non-breaking space

(in word-processing or DTP software) space character that prevents two words being separated by a line break

non-interlaced

(in a monitor) system in which the picture electron beam scans each line of the display once during each refresh cycle; the beam in an interlaced display scans every alternate line

nonlinear video editing

method of editing a video sequence in which the video is digitized and stored in a computer; the editor can then cut and move frames in any order before outputing the finished sequence. The finished sequence can either be produced directly from the computer output - but this is normally at a lower quality than the original due to compression losses, or the computer can output timecode instructions that can be used to edit the original video tape

nonmodal

(in a GUI) displaying a window but still allowing a user to access other windows that are on-screen before closing the nonmodal window

compare with

MODAL

non-scrollable

(part of the screen display) which is always displayed (in a WP, the text can scroll while the menu bar or status line are always visible

notification message

message within authoring software to notify other objects that a particular task has been completed; for example, if an object is moved, the application will generate a notification message to tell other processes when it has finished moving the object

notify handler

series of commands that are executed when a particular notification message is received; for example, the programmer could create a notify handler to carry out a task when it receives a message from a button object that says it has been selected with the mouse pointer

Novell™

large company that produces network software; it is best known for its NetWare™ range of network operating system software that runs on a PC server; it also produces AppWare™, a visual object-oriented application programming system

ns

NANOSECOND

NTSC

NATIONAL TELEVISION STANDARDS COMMITTEE

NuBus

high-speed 96-pin expansion bus used within a Modular Apple Macintosh computer

null string

string that contains no characters

null terminated string

string of characters that has a null character to indicate the end of the string

Oo

object
(i) the data that makes up a particular image or sound; (ii) variable used in an expert system within a reasoning operation; (iii) data in a statement which is to be operated on by the operator

object *or* object-orientated architecture
structure where all files, outputs, etc., in a system are represented as objects

object animation
see
CAST-BASED ANIMATION

object hierarchy
order in which messages are passed from one object to another

object linking and embedding (OLE)
(in Microsoft Windows) method of sharing data between applications; an object (such as an image or sound) can be linked to a document or spreadsheet; the application that creates the document that holds an embedded object is the client application, whereas the application that creates the object that is embedded is called the server application - confusingly, an application can be both client and server
see also
EMBEDDING, LINKING, OBJECT PACKAGER

object-oriented

(system or language) that uses objects which respond to messages from the system (such as a mouse click) or from other objects

object-oriented graphics

image which uses vector definitions (lines, curves) to describe the shapes of the image rather than pixels in a bit-map image

object-oriented language

programming language that is used for object-oriented programming, such as C++

object-oriented programming (OOP)

method of programming, such as C++, in which each element of the program is treated as an object that can interact with other objects within the program

Object Packager™

Microsoft Windows utility that combines a data file with information about the application that created it so that the combined package can be inserted into another application
see also
OLE

OCE

OPEN COLLABORATION ENVIRONMENT
set of standards that allow networked Macintosh users to share objects and files

OCR

OPTICAL CHARACTER READER
device which scans printed or written characters, recognizes them, and converts them into machine-readable form for processing in a computer

OCR

OPTICAL CHARACTER RECOGNITION
(software) process that allows printed or written characters to be recognized optically and converted into machine-readable code that can be input into a computer, using an optical character reader

OCR font

character design that can be easily read using an OCR reader; there are two OCR fonts in common use: OCR-A, which is easy for scanners to read, and OCR-B, which is easier for people to read than the OCR-A font

OEM

ORIGINAL EQUIPMENT MANUFACTURER

company which produces equipment using basic parts made by other manufacturers, and customizes the product for a particular application

off-line editing

editing process in which copies of the original sound or video tape are used, cut, edited to create an EDL that is then used in an on-line editing suite to automatically assemble all the sectors of the tape according to the instructions in the EDL

Off-line editing software allows two or more video clips to be edited and merged with effects.

off-screen buffer

area of RAM used to hold an off-screen image before it is displayed on screen

off-screen image

image that is first drawn into a memory area and then is transferred to the display memory

OK

used as a prompt in place of 'ready' in some systems

OK button

(in a GUI) button with 'OK' label that is used to start or confirm an action

OLE

OBJECT LINKING AND EMBEDDING

(in Microsoft Windows) method of sharing data between applications; an object (such as an image or sound) can be linked to a document or spreadsheet; the application that creates the document that holds an embedded object is the client application, wheras the application that creates the object that is embedded is called the server application - confusingly, an application can be both client and server
see also
EMBEDDING, LINKING, OBJECT PACKAGER

183

OLE-2

(in Windows) extends the functions of OLE to include visual editing to allow the embedded object to be edited without leaving the document in which it is embedded; also drag-and-drop functions to place embedded objects

OLE container object

object that contains a reference to a linked object or a copy of an embedded object

OMR

see
OPTICAL MARK READER

OMR

see
OPTICAL MARK RECOGNITION

online *or* on-line

state when a peripheral (such as a printer) is ready to receive data and process it

on-line editing

process of creating a finished audio or film sequence from original tape using editing instructions in an EDL list

on-line help

help text provided within an application about a function

on-screen

(information) that is displayed on a computer screen rather than printed out on paper

on the fly

(to examine and modify data) during a program run without stopping the run

OOP

OBJECT ORIENTED PROGRAMMING

O/P *or* o/p

OUTPUT

open

(command) to prepare a file before reading or writing actions can occur

Open Collaboration Environment (OCE)
set of standards that allow networked Macintosh users to share objects and files

open file
file that can be read from or written to; the application opens the file on disk and prepares it for an operation

OpenScript™
object-oriented programming language used in Asymetrix' Toolbook authoring software

operand
data (within a computer program instruction) which is to be operated on by the operator

operating system (OS)
software that controls the basic, low-level hardware operations, and file management, without the user having to operate it (the operating system is usually supplied with the computer as part of the bundled software) for example, MS-DOS on a PC or System 7.5 on a Macintosh; NOTE: Windows 3.1 is not an operating system, it is a GUI shell, wheras Windows 95 is an operating system with a GUI front-end

operator
character or symbol or word that defines a function or an operation; for example, 'x' is the multiplication operator

operator overloading
assigning more than one function to a particular operator (the function often depends on the type of data being operated on and is used in the C++ and Ada programming languages)

operator precedence
order in which a number of mathematical operations will be carried out

optical bar reader *or* bar code reader *or* optical wand
optical device that reads data from a bar code

optical character reader (OCR)
device which scans printed or written characters, recognizes them, and converts them into machine-readable code for processing in a computer

optical character recognition (OCR)

(software) process that allows printed or written characters to be recognized optically and converted into machine-readable code that can be input into a computer, using an optical character reader

optical disk

disk that contains binary data in the form of small holes in a metal layer under the surface, which are read with a laser beam; NOTE: also called WORM (write once, read many times) which can be programmed once, or compact disk (CD) which is programmed at manufacture

optical fibre

fine strand of glass or plastic protected by a surrounding material, that is used for the convenient transmission of light signals

optical font *or* OCR font

character design that can be easily read using an OCR reader; there are two OCR fonts in common use: OCR-A, which is easy for scanners to read, and OCR-B, which is easier for people to read than the OCR-A font

optical mark reader (OMR)

device that can recognize marks or lines on a special forms (such as on an order form or a reply to a questionnaire) and convert them into a form a computer can process

optical mark recognition (OMR)

process that allows certain marks or lines on special forms (such as on an order form or a reply to a questionnaire) to be recognized by an optical mark reader, and input into a computer

optical mouse

pointing device that is operated by moving it across a special flat mat; on the mat is printed a grid of lines; as the mouse is moved, two light sensors count the number of lines that have been passed to produce a measure of the distance and direction of travel; an optical mouse has fewer moving parts than a mechanical mouse and so is more reliable, but requires an accurately printed mat
compare with
MECHANICAL MOUSE

optical scanner

equipment that converts an image into electrical signals which can be stored in and displayed on a computer

186

optical wand

see
OPTICAL BAR READER

optimization

making something work as efficiently as possible

optimized code

program that has had any inefficient code or statements removed to make it run faster or to use less memory

optimizing compiler

compiler that analyses the machine code it produces in order to improve the speed or efficiency of the code

option

one action or member of a list which can be chosen by a user

Option key

(on an Apple Macintosh) key on the keyboard that gives access to secondary functions of keys; similar to Ctrl or Alt keys on an IBM PC keyboard, located to the left of the space bar

Orange Book

set of standards published by Philips that define the format for a recordable CD-ROM
see also
GREEN BOOK, RED BOOK, YELLOW BOOK, WHITE BOOK

orientation

(i) direction or position of an object; (ii) (in word-processing or DTP software) direction of a page, either landscape (long edge horizontal) or portrait (long edge vertical)

origin

(i) position on a display screen to which all coordinates are referenced, usually the top left hand corner of the screen; (ii) location in memory at which the first instruction of a program is stored

original

used first or made first; for example, if you scan in a photograph, the photograph is the original

original equipment manufacturer (OEM)

company which produces equipment using basic parts made by other manufacturers, and customizes the product for a particular application

orphan

first line of a paragraph of text printed alone at the bottom of a column, with the rest of the paragraph at the top of the next column; an orphan makes a page look ugly
compare
WIDOW

OS

OPERATING SYSTEM
software that controls the basic, low-level hardware operations, and file management, without the user having to operate it (the operating system is usually supplied with the computer as part of the bundled software; for example, MS-DOS on a PC or System 7.5 on a Macintosh) NOTE: Windows 3.1 is not an operating system, it is a GUI shell, wheras Windows 95 is an operating system with a GUI front-end

OS/2™

multitasking operating system for PC computers originally developed by IBM and Microsoft, now development is carried out by IBM; OS/2 provides a 32-bit software kernel with both a graphical user interface (called Presentation Manager) and a command line; the newest version, called OS/2 WARP, can run Microsoft Windows 3.1 applications under the OS/2 operating system

outline font

printer or display font (collection of characters) stored as a set of outlines that mathematically describe the shape of each character (which are then used to draw each character rather than actual patterns of dots); outline fonts can be easily scaled, unlike bit-mapped fonts
see also
BIT-MAPPED FONTS

output

information or data that is transferred from a computer to a peripheral device, such as a printer

overdub

to record a new voice or sound to replace an existing sound on a film or video

overlay

(i) strip of paper that is placed above keys on a keyboard to indicate their function; (ii) small section of a program; the entire program is bigger than the main memory capacity of a computer, and so the overlay is loaded into memory when required, so that main memory only contains the sections it requires; (iii) device that converts composite video or television signals into a digital format so that they can be displayed on a computer

overlay function
see
MATTE, CHROMA KEY

overscan
(i) faulty or badly adjusted monitor in which the displayed image runs off the edge of the screen; (ii) display equipment in which the picture beam scans past of the screen boundaries to ensure that the image fills the screen

overwrite
writing text or data over existing text or data, destroying the original

Pp

P-code
intermediate code produced by a compiler that is ready for an interpreter to process, usually for PASCAL programs

pack
to store a quantity of data in a reduced form, often by representing several characters of data with one stored character

paddle
computer peripheral consisting of a knob or device which is turned to move a cursor or a pointer on the screen

page
(i) amount of text displayed on a computer monitor or screen (which if printed out would fill a page of paper which fills the screen); (ii) blank area of the screen used as a background for a multimedia book; the design of each page is created by pasting objects, such as a windows, buttons, graphic images and text onto the page; (iii) (normally) 24 lines of text that fill a screen (not as it will print out on papaer)

page break
(i) point at which a page ends and a new page starts (in continuous text); (ii) marker used (in word-processing) to show where a new page should start

page description language (PDL)
software that controls a printer's actions to print a page of text to a particular format, according to a user's instructions
see also
PCL, POSTSCRIPT

page display
showing on the screen a page of text as it will appear when printed out

page down key *or* PgDn
(on a keyboard) key that moves the cursor position down by the number of lines on one screen

page image buffer
memory in a page printer that holds the image as it is built up before it is printed

page layout
arrangement of text and pictures within a page of a document

page length
length of a page (in word-processing)

page makeup
action of pasting images and text into a page ready for printing

page number
unique number assigned to each page within a multimedia application, to be used within hyperlinks and when moving between pages

page orientation
direction of the long edge of a piece of paper
see
PORTRAIT, LANDSCAPE

pages per minute (ppm)
number of pages that a printer can print in one minute; measurement of the speed of a printer shown as the number of pages of text printed every minute

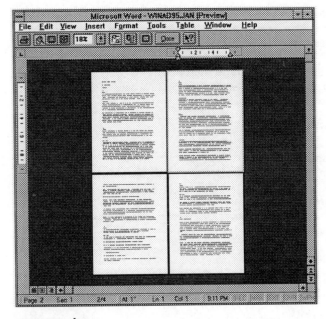

Microsoft Word includes a page-preview feature that allows the user to see how the printed pages will look.

page preview

(in WP or DTP software) graphical representation of how a page will look when printed, with different type styles, margins, and graphics correctly displayed

page printer

printer which composes one page of text within memory and then prints it in one pass (normally refers to laser printers)

page setup

(within software) options that allow a user to set up how the page will look when printed - setting the margins, size of paper, and scaling of a page

page up key *or* PgUp

(on a keyboard) key that moves the cursor position up by the number of lines in one screen

page addressing

main memory which has been split into blocks, with a unique address allocated to each block of memory, which can then be called up and accessed individually when required

page-mode RAM

dynamic RAM designed to access sequential memory locations very quickly

paged-memory scheme

way of dividing memory into areas (pages) which are then allocated a page number; memory addresses are relative to a page which is then mapped to the real, physical memory (this is normally used to implement virtual memory)

pagination

process of dividing text into pages; arrangement of pages in a book

paint

to fill an area with colour or draw pictures on screen

paint object

bitmap image

paint program

software that allows a user to draw pictures on screen in different colours, with different styles of brush and special effects; paint programs normally operate on bitmap images; drafting or design software normally works with vector-based images

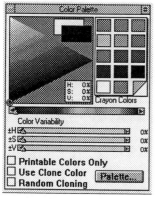

Paint programs include sophisticated palette control.

PAL

PHASE ALTERNATION LINE

standard for television transmission and reception using a 625-line picture transmitted at 25 frames per second; PAL provides a clearer image than NTSC and is used in most of Europe, except for France which uses SECAM. The USA and Japan use NTSC

palette
(i) range of colours which can be used (on a printer or computer display); (ii) (in Windows) data structure that defines the colours used in a bitmap image; the palette data defines each colour, the bitmap includes references to the colours in the palette

palette shift
image displayed using the wrong palette so that the colours appear distorted

pan
(i) (in computer graphics) to smoothly move a viewing window horizontally across an image that is too wide to display all at once; (ii) (in MIDI or sound) to adjust the balance of a sound between the two stereo channels; (iii) to smoothly move a camera horizontally

Pantone Matching System™ (PMS)
standard method of matching ink colours on screen and on printed output using a book of pre-defined colours

paper
another term for the background of an image onto which the image is drawn

paper-white monitor
monitor that normally displays black text on a white background, rather than the normal illuminated text on a black background

paragraph
(in a document) section of text between two carriage return characters

paragraph marker
(in a document) non-printing character that shows where a carriage return is within a document

parallel port
connector on a computer or peripheral that allows several bits of data to be transmitted simultaneously, normally eight bits at a time

parallel printer
printer that is connected to a computer via a parallel interface and accepts character data in parallel form (eight bits at a time sent over eight wires)

parameter
information which defines the limits or actions of something, such as a variable

or routine or program

parameter passing
(in a program) value passed to a routine or program when it is called

parametric equalizer
device that can enhance or reduce the levels of particular frequencies within an audio signal; used to remove distorsion from a signal and cut out excessive bass or high-pitch noise from an audio signal

parent directory
(in DOS filing system) the directory above a sub-directory

parent folder
(in Macintosh filing system) one folder that contains other folders

parent program
program that starts another program (a child program), whilst it is still running; control passes back to the parent program when the child program has finished

parent object
page that contains the object that is being referenced

parts per quarter note
see
PPQN

passage
a number of notes that form a small section of a musical score

paste
to insert text or graphics that has been copied or cut into a file; cut-and-paste is a feature common in most GUIs; it allows the user to take a section of text or data from one point and insert it at another (often used in word-processors and DTP packages for easy page editing)

patch
(i) (temporary) correction made to a program; small correction made to software by the user, on the instructions of the software publisher; (ii) data that defines a sound in a synthesizer; a patch is also called a program and can be altered by issuing a program-change message

patch cord
short cable with a connector at each end, used to make an electrical connection on a patch panel

patch panel
unit with electrical terminals that can be interconnected using short patch cords, allowing quick and simple re-configuration between musical instruments or other devices

path
(in the DOS operating system) list of subdirectories where the operating system should look for a named file

pattern
series of regular lines or shapes which are repeated again and again

pattern palette
range of predefined patterns that can be used to fill an area of an image

pattern recognition
algorithms or program functions that can identify a shape from a video camera, etc.

PC
PERSONAL COMPUTER
(originally referring to a microcomputer specification with an 8086-based low-power computer); now normally used to refer to any computer that uses an Intel 80x86 processor and is based on the IBM PC-style architecture

PC-compatible
computer that is compatible with the IBM PC

PC AT
(IBM PC compatible) computer that used an Intel 80286 processor and was fitted with 16-bit ISA expansion connectors

PC AT keyboard
keyboard with twelve function keys arranged in one row along the top of the keyboard

PC display modes
see
APPENDIX: GRAPHICS MODES

196

PC XT

(IBM PC compatible) computer that was fitted with a hard disk drive and used a 8086 Intel processor

PC XT keyboard

keyboard with ten function keys arranged in two columns along the left hand side of the keyboard

PCI

PERIPHERAL COMPONENT INTERCONNECT

hardware specification, produced by Intel, defining a type of fast local bus that allows high-speed data transfer between the processor and a peripheral or expansion cards (normally a video adapter, disk controller or network card); the PCI bus can work with either an ISA or EISA expansion bus system and runs at 33MHz with either 32 or 64-bit data path between the CPU and the peripheral

PCL™

PRINTER CONTROL LANGUAGE

standard set of commands, defined by Hewlett Packard, that allow a computer to control a printer

PCM

PULSE-CODE MODULATION

method of digitizing sound by sampling the sound signal at regular intervals (often 8 or 16 thousand times per second) and converting the level of the signal into a number; normally the sample rate is twice the maximum frequency of the signal - for example, a 4KHz signal would be sampled 8,000 times per second to preserve the detail of the original signal

PCM

PLUG-COMPATIBLE MANUFACTURER

company that produces add-on boards which are compatible with another manufacturer's computer

PCMCIA™

PERSONAL COMPUTER MEMORY CARD INTERNATIONAL ASSOCIATION
specification for add-in expansion cards that are the size of a credit card with a connector at one end

PCMCIA card

memory or peripheral which complies with the PCMCIA standard

PCMCIA connector

68-pin connector that is inside a PCMCIA slot and on the end of a PCMCIA card

PCMCIA slot

expansion slot (normally on a laptop) that can accept a PCMCIA expansion card

PCX

standard file format for storing colour graphics images

PDA

PERSONAL DIGITAL ASSISTANT

lightweight palmtop computer that provides the basic functions of a diary, notepad, address-book and to-do list together with fax or modem communications; current PDA designs do not have a keyboard, but use a touch-sensitive screen with a pen and handwriting-recognition to control the software; the Apple Newton is one of the current range of PDAs available

PDL

PAGE DESCRIPTION LANGUAGE, PROGRAM DESIGN LANGUAGE

pel

PICTURE ELEMENT

the smallest area on a screen that can be individually controlled - note that this is not necessarily the same as a pixel, since a pel could be made up of several pixels

Pentium™

processor developed by Intel; it is backwards compatible with the 80x86 family used in IBM PCs; the processor uses a 32-bit address bus and a 64-bit data bus

peripheral

(i) item of hardware (such as terminals, printers, monitors, etc.) which is attached to a main computer system; (ii) any device that allows communication between a system and itself, but is not directly operated by the system

peripheral component interconnect

see
PCI

permanent swap file

file on a hard disk, made up of contiguous disk sectors, which stores a swap file for software that implements virtual memory, such as Microsoft's Windows; NOTE: Windows supports either permanent or temporary swap files, but a permanent file is faster

persistence

length of time that a CRT will continue to display an image after the picture beam has stopped tracing it on the screen

personal computer

see
PC

Personal Computer Memory Card International Association

see
PCMCIA

personal digital assistant

see
PDA

perspective

appearance of depth in an image in which objects that are further away from the viewer appear smaller

PgDn

see
PAGE DOWN KEY

PgUp

see
PAGE UP KEY

phase alternation line (PAL)

standard for television transmission and reception using a 625-line picture transmitted at 25 frames per second; PAL provides a clearer image than NTSC and is used in most of Europe, except for France which uses SECAM. The USA and Japan use NTSC

PHIGS

PROGRAMMER'S HIERARCHICAL INTERACTIVE GRAPHICS STANDARD
standard application interface between software and a graphics adapter that

uses a set of standard commands to draw and manipulate 2D and 3D images

phoneme
one small sound, several of which may make up a spoken word; used to analyse voice input to recognise words or to produce speech by playing back a sequence of phonemes

phono connector or RCA connector
plug and socket standard used to connect audio and video devices; the male plug has a 1/8-inch metal central core that sticks out from within the centre of an insulated core

phosphor
substance that produces light when excited by some form of energy, usually an electron beam, used for coating the inside of a cathode ray tube; a thin layer of phosphor is arranged in a pattern of small dots on the inside of a television screen and produces an image when scanned by the picture beam
see
TELEVISION

phosphor coating
thin layer of phosphor on the inside of a CRT screen

phosphor dots
individual dots of red, green and blue phosphor on a colour CRT screen

phosphor efficiency
measure of the amount of light produced in ratio to the energy received from an electron beam

photodigital memory
computer memory system that uses a LASER to write data onto a piece of film which can then be read many times but not written to again; NOTE: also called WORM (Write Once Read Many times memory)

PhotoCD™
standard of storing 35mm photographic slides or negatives in digital format on a CD-ROM. The Photo CD is normally created at the same time as the photographic film is developed - by digitizing each frame at a resolution of 2048x3072 pixels with 24bit colour (together with a lower-resolution preview image file); one Photo CD can hold 100 photographs. To read a Photo CD disc, the CD-ROM drive must conform to the CD-ROM XA standard. If all the images are recorded onto the Photo CD at the same time, then the disc can

be read by a single-session drive; if further images are recorded onto the Photo CD at a later date, then the disc can only be read by a multi-session CD-ROM drive; developed by Kodak and Philips

photorealistic

digital computer image that has almost the same quality and clarity as a photograph; for example, images stored on a Photo CD are photorealistic since they are scanned at a resolution of 2048x3072 pixels in 24-bit colour

phototypesetter

device that can produce very high-resolution text on photo-sensitive paper or film; the phototypesetter, rather like a large laser printer, normally uses the PostScript page description language and can generate type at 2,540 dpi; if the device is capable of outputting text and half-tone images, it is normally called an image setter

PIC

PICTURE IMAGE COMPRESSION
image compression algorithm used in Intel's DVI video system
see also
DVI

PIC

PICTURE
method of storing vector graphic images, developed by Lotus for its 1-2-3 spreadsheet charts and graphs

pica

(i) measurment equal to 12points (0.166 inch); (ii) width of characters in a typeface, usually 12 characters to the inch

pickup

graph showing the sensitivity of a microphone according to the direction of the source; the two most common patterns are omni-directional (the microphone will pick up sound from any direction) and uni-directional (the microphone is focussed and responds to sound from one direction only)

pickup reel

empty reel used to take the tape as it is played from a full reel

PICS

file format used to import a sequence of PICT files on a Macintosh

PICT
PICTURE
(Apple Macintosh) graphics file format that stores images in the QuickDraw vector format

picture
printed or drawn image of an object or scene

picture beam
moving electron beam in a TV, that produces an image on the screen by illuminating the phosphor coating and by varying its intensity according to the received signal

picture element *or* pixel
smallest single unit or point on a display whose colour or brightness can be controlled
see also
PIXEL, PEL

picture image compression
see
PIC

picture level benchmark
see
PLB

picture object
an image created with a vector drawing package and stored as vectors rather than as a bitmap

picture processing
analysis of information contained in an image, usually by computer or electronic methods, providing analysis or recognition of objects in the image

PIF
see
PROGRAM INFORMATION FILE

pinchwheel
small rubber wheel in a tape machine that holds the tape in place and prevents flutter

pincushion distorsion

distorsion of an image displayed on a monitor in which the edges curve in towards the centre

pipelining

(i) method of executing several instructions in parallel to increase performance; (ii) to carry out more than one task at a time: for example, to compress and store an image on disk as it is being scanned

pitch

(i) number of characters which will fit into one inch of line, when the characters are typed in single spacing (used on line-printers, the normal pitches available being 10, 12 and 17 characters per inch); (ii) frequency of a sound

pitch scale factor

instruction to a waveform audio device to change the pitch of the sound by a factor; a factor of two is equal to an increase in pitch of one octave and requires complex sound hardware to carry this out without changing the sample rate or playback rate

pix

picture or pictures

pixel *or* picture element

smallest single unit or point on a display; in high resolution display systems the colour or brightness of a single pixel can be controlled; in low resolution systems a group of pixels are controlled at the same time
see also
CRT, PEL, RESOLUTION
> APPENDIX: PC GRAPHICS

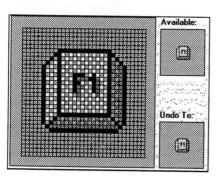

The larger image shows how individual pixels make up an icon.

plane
(in a graphics image) one layer of an image that can be manipulated independently within a graphics program

plasma display *or* gas plasma display
display screen using the electroluminescing properties of certain gases to display text; this is a thin display usually used in small portable computers
compare with
LCD

platform
standard type of hardware that makes up a particular range of computers

platform independence
software that can work with different types of incompatible hardware

playback
running a multimedia title or view a video clip or listening to a recorded sound

play back
to read data or a signal from a recording medium

playback head
transducer that reads signals recorded on a storage medium and usually converts them to an electrical signal

playback rate scale factor
(i) (in waveform audio) sound played back at a different rate, directed by another application, to create a special effect - created by skipping samples rather than changing the sample rate; (ii) (video displayed on a computer) point at which video playback is no longer smooth and appears jerky due to missed frames; this is determined by the size of the playback window and the power of the processor

player missile graphics
see
SPRITES

PLB
PICTURE LEVEL BENCHMARK
benchmark used to measure the performance (not the quality) of a graphics adapter or workstation

plot

to draw an image (especially a graph) as short lines between two points, based on information supplied as a series of coordinates; used to print vector images rather than bitmap images

plotter

computer peripheral that draws straight lines between two coordinates; plotters are used for graph and diagram plotting and can plot curved lines as a number of short straight lines

plug-compatible

equipment manufactured to operate with another system when connected to it by a connector or cable

plug-compatible manufacturer

see
PCM

PLV

PRODUCTION LEVEL VIDEO

highest-quality video compression algorithm used with DVI full-motion video sequences; the compression is around 120:1 and is carried out off-line once the video has been recorded - the compressed data can be decompressed in real time during playback

PMS

see
PANTONE MATCHING SYSTEM

point

(i) to move an on-screen cursor using a mouse or arrow keys; (ii) (typography) a unit of measurement equal to 1/72-inch - normally used to measure the height of a character

point size

(typography) a unit of measurement equal to 1/72-inch - it indicates the height of a character

pointer

(i) variable in a computer program that contains the address to a data item or instruction; (ii) graphical symbol used to indicate the position of a cursor on a display; a pointer is normally an arrow, but changes to an I-beam when editing

pointing device

input device that controls the position of a cursor on screen as it is moved by the user
see also
MOUSE; TABLET

polar coordinates

system of defining positions as an angle and distance from the origin
compare
CARTESIAN COORDINATES

polygon

graphics shape with three or more sides

pop-down menu *or* pop-up menu

menu that can be displayed on the screen at any time by pressing the appropriate key, usually displayed over material already on the screen; once the user has made a choice from the menu, it disappears and the original screen display is restored

pop-up window

window that can be displayed on the screen at any time on top of anything that is already on the screen; when the window is removed, the original screen display is restored
see also
WINDOW, MODAL

port

(i) to transfer an application between platforms; (ii) communications channel that allows a computer to exchange data with a peripheral

portable

(i) compact self-contained computer that can be carried around and used either with a battery pack or mains power supply; (ii) (any hardware or software or data files) that can used on a range of different computers

portable operating system interface

see
POSIX

portable software *or* portable programs

programs that can be run on several different computer systems

portrait
orientation of a page or piece of paper where the longest edge is vertical
compare
LANDSCAPE

positive display
(screen) where the text and graphics are shown as black on a white background to imitate a printed page

POSIX
PORTABLE OPERATING SYSTEM INTERFACE
IEEE standard that defines a set of services provided by an operating system; software that works to the POSIX standard can be easily ported between hardware platforms

post production
final editing process of a video or animation in which titles are added and sequences finalised

PostScript™
standard page description language developed by Adobe Systems; PostScript offers flexible font sizing and positioning; it is most often used in DTP systems, high-quality laser printers and phototypesetters; Display PostScript is an extension of PostScript that allows PostScript commands to be displayed on a screen so that a user can see exactly what will appear on the printer; an Encapsulated PostScript file contains PostScript commands that describe an image or page, the commands are stored in a file and this can be placed on a page; an encapsulated PostScript file often contains a preview image in TIFF or PICT format

PowerCD™
CD-ROM player produced by Apple that can connect to a television to display Photo CD images, or to a Macintosh as a standard CD-ROM drive, or to play back music CDs

PowerPC™
RISC-based processor developed by Motorola and used in the PowerPC range of Apple Macintosh computers

power user
user who needs the latest, fastest model of computer because he runs complex or demanding applications

PowerBook™
laptop version of a Macintosh computer, designed by Apple and compatible with the desktop models; includes mono or colour screen, hard disk drive, keyboard and either a built-in trackball or touch-sensitive pad to control the position of the mouse

ppm
PAGES PER MINUTE

PPQN
PARTS PER QUARTER NOTE
most common time format used with standard MIDI sequences

pre-amplifier
electronic circuit which amplifies a signal to a particular level, before it is fed to an amplifier for output

precedence
computational rules defining the order in which mathematical operations are calculated (usually multiplications are done first, then divisions, additions, and subtractions last)

preemptive multitasking
form of multitasking in which the operating system executes a program for a period of time, then passes control to the next program so preventing any one program using all the processor time; this is a feature of IBM OS/2 and should be part of Microsoft Windows 95

pre-fetch
CPU instructions stored in a short temporary queue before being processed, increasing the speed of execution; often used to speed up processing of complex image files

pre-imaging
to generate one frame of an animation or video in a memory buffer before it is transferred on-screen for display

pre-production
stage before a video or interactive title is edited when media is collected and the title designed

prescan
feature of many flat-bed scanners and control software that carry out a quick,

low-resolution scan to allow the operator to re-position the original or mark the area that is to be scanned at a higher resolution

presentation graphics
graphics used to represent business information or data

Presentation Manager™
graphical user interface supplied with the OS/2 operating system, similar to Windows, but includes slightly different utilities

presentation software
software application that allows a user to create a business presentation with graphs, data, text and images

preview
to display text or graphics on a screen as it will appear when it is printed out

previewer
feature that allows a user to see on screen what a page will look like when printed

primitive
(i) (in programming) basic routine that can be used to create more complex routines; (ii) (in graphics) simple shape (such as circle, square, line, curve) used to create more complex shapes in a graphics program

print
characters created with ink or toner on paper

print control character
special character sent to a printer that directs it to perform an action or function (such as change font), rather than print a character

printer
device that produces text or image on paper using ink or tonerunder the control of a computer; there are many different kinds of printer: a daisy-wheel printer is an impact printer that strikes an inked ribbon with characters arranged on interchangeable daisy-wheels; a dot-matrix printer forms characters from a series of tiny dots printed close together; an ink-jet printer produces characters by sending a stream of tiny drops of electrically charged ink onto the paper (the movement of the ink drops is controlled by an electric field); a laser printer is a high-resolution printer that uses a laser source to print high quality dot-matrix characters normally at a resolution of 300 or

600dpi; a line-printer prints text one character at a time, moving horizontally across each line; a page printer composes one page of text, then prints it rapidly (such as a laser printer)
see also
INK-JET, LASER, THERMAL-WAX PRINTER

printer buffer
temporary store for character data waiting to be printed (used to free the computer before the printing is completed making the operation faster)

printer control language
see
PCL

printer driver
software that converts output from an application to control codes for a printer

printer emulation
printer that is able to interpret the standard set of commands used to control another brand of printer

printhead
(i) row of needles in a dot-matrix printer that produce characters as a pattern of dots; (ii) metal form of a character that is pressed onto an inked ribbon to print the character on paper

print job
file in a print queue that contains all the characters and printer control codes needed to print one document or page

print life
number of characters a component can print before needing to be replaced

print modifiers
codes in a document that cause a printer to change mode, i.e. from bold to italic

printout
final printed page

print preview
function of a software product that lets the user see how a page will appear when printed

print queue
area of memory that stores print jobs ready to send to the printer when it has finished its current work

print server
computer in a network that is dedicated to managing print queues and printers

print spooling
automatic printing of a number of different documents in a queue at the normal speed of the printer, while the computer is doing some other task

PRN
PRINTER
acronym used in MS-DOS to represent the standard printer port

procedure
small section of computer instruction code that provides a frequently used function and can be called upon from a main program

production level video
see
PLV

program
(i) complete set of instructions which direct a computer to carry out a particular task; (ii) (in MIDI) data that defines a sound in a synthesizer; a program is also called a patch and can be altered by issuing a program-change message

program generator
software that allows users to write complex programs using a few simple instructions

program icon
(in a GUI) icon that represents an executable program file

program information file (PIF)
(in Microsoft Windows) file that contains the environment settings for a particular program

program instruction
single word or expression that represents one operation (in a high level program each program instruction can consist of a number of low level machine code instructions)

program item
(in a GUI) an icon that represents a program

programmer's hierachical interactive graphics standard
see
PHIGS

programming language
software that allows a user to write a series of instructions to define a particular task, which will then be translated to a form that is understood by the computer; programming languages are grouped into different levels: the high-level languages such as BASIC and PASCAL are easy to understand and use, but offer slow execution time since each instruction is made up of a number of machine code instructions; low-level languages (such as assembler) are more complex to read and program in, but offer faster execution time

prompt
message or character displayed to remind the user that an input is expected; for example, the command prompt is a symbol displayed to indicate a command is expected

properties
attributes of an object that define its appearance and behaviour, such as its position, colour, shape, and name

proportional spacing
printing system where each letter takes a space proportional to the character width ('i' taking less space than 'm')
compare
MONOSPACING

protected mode
operating mode of an Intel processor (the 80286 or higher) that supports multitasking, virtual memory, and data security
compare
REAL MODE

prototyping
creating the first working model of a device or program, which is then tested and adapted to improve it

PrtSc
PRINT SCREEN

(on an IBM PC keyboard) key that sends the contents of the current screen to the printer

PS/2™

range of IBM PC computers that are software compatible with the original IBM PC, but use a different MCA expansion bus
see also
MCA

public domain (PD)

documents or images or sound or text or program that has no copying fee or restrictions and can be used or copied by anyone
compare
SHAREWARE

publish

(i) to produce and sell software; (ii) to design edit, print and sell books or magazines; computers and multimedia have greatly influenced how works are published: desktop publishing (DTP) is the design, layout and printing of documents using special software, a small computer and a printer, while electronic publishing uses computers to write and display information (such as viewdata or CD-ROM titles); (iii) to share a local resource with other users on a network (such as a file or folder)

pull-down menu

set of options that are displayed below the relevant entry on a menu-bar

pulse-code modulation (PCM)

see
PCM, ADPCM

push-button

square shape displayed on a screen that will carry out a particular action if selected with a pointer or keyboard; a push-button is normally made up of two images: one displayed with shading to appear as if it is protruding from the screen and a second, displayed when the user selects the button, that is shaded differently to appear to sink into the screen

Qq

Q Channel

(in a CD audio disc) one of the eight information channels that holds data indentifying the track and the absolute playing time

QAM

QUADRATURE AMPLITUDE MODULATION

quad-speed drive

CD-ROM drive that spins the disc at four times the speed of a single-speed drive, providing higher data throughput of 600Kbps and shorter seek times

quadrature amplitude modulation (QAM)

data encoding method used by high-speed modems (transmitting at rates above 2,400bps); QAM combines amplitude modulation and phase modulation to increase the data transmission rate

quadrature encoding

system used to determine the direction in which a mouse is being moved; in a mechanical mouse, two sensors send signals that describe its horizontal and vertical movements - these signals are transmitted using quadrature encoding

214

Quantel™

hardware graphics company that developed Paintbox and Harry production graphics systems

quantize

(i) to convert an analog signal into a numerical representation; (ii) to process a MIDI file and align all the notes to a regular beat, so removing any timing errors

quantizer

device used to convert an analog input signal to a numerical form that can be processed by a computer

quantization

conversion of an analog signal to a numerical representation

quantization error

error in converting an analog signal into a numerical form due to limited accuracy or rapidly changing signal
see also
A/D

quantizing noise

noise on a signal due to inaccuracies in the quantizing process

query message

message sent to an object to find out the value of one of the object's properties, such as its name, active state or position (used in authoring languages to determine, for example, if a checkbox has been selected)

query window

(i) window that appears when an error has occured, asking the user what action he would like to take; (ii) window that is displayed with fields a user can fill in to search a database

QuickDraw™

(in an Apple Macintosh) graphics routines built into the Macintosh's operating system that control displayed text and images

QuickTime™

(in an Apple Macintosh) video and sound routines built into the Macintosh's System 7 operating system that allow windows, boxes and graphic objects (including animation and video files) to be displayed; a QuickTime file can contain 32 tracks of audio, video, or MIDI data. QuickTime is also available as an add-on driver for Microsoft Windows PC environments; normally plays video at 15 frames per second

QWERTY keyboard

English language keyboard layout for a typewriter or computer, in which the top line of letters are QWERTY

Rr

radio button

(in a GUI) circle displayed beside an option that, when selected, has a dark centre; radio buttons are a method of selecting one of a number of options, only one radio button can be selected at one time (select another and the first is deselected)
see also
BUTTON, PUSH BUTTON

radio frequency (RF)

electromagnetic spectrum that lies between the frequency range 10KHz and 3000GHz

ragged

not straight or with an uneven edge

ragged left

printed text with a flush right-hand margin and uneven left-hand margin

ragged right

printed text with a flush left-hand margin and uneven right-hand margin

ragged text

unjustified text, text with a ragged right margin

Useful Tips and Tricks

One of the benefits of networking Windows for Workgroups is that everyone can share data; this is great, unless you want to keep particular files private and secure. Of course, you could place sensitive files in a separate directory and remove the share rights for this directory.

Sometimes, this isn't practical and you need to protect files - such as backup password lists, budgets or reports - in a common directory. File Locker is a neat Windows shareware utility that will encrypt files (and you can use wildcards) with a password to prevent anyone else reading their contents. It's available as WINLOCK.ZIP on CompuServe or CIX.

The first line is centred, the first paragraph is ragged right and the second paragraph is ragged left.

RAM

RANDOM ACCESS MEMORY

memory that allows access to any location in any order, without having to access the rest first (the memory chips in your PC are RAM, since any location can be accessed by specifying its address; a magnetic tape is not random access, since you must read through all locations before you reach the one you want to access)

RAM cache

section of high-speed RAM that is used to buffer data transfers between the (faster) processor and a (slower) disk drive

random access memory

see
RAM

range left

move text to align it to the left margin

raster

system of scanning the whole of a CRT screen with a picture beam by sweeping across it horizontally, moving down one pixel or line at a time

raster graphics

graphics where the picture is built up in lines across the screen or page

raster image processor (RIP)

computer which translates software instructions into an image or complete page which is then printed by a printer or imagesetter (often used to speed up typesetting images)

raster scan

one sweep of the picture beam horizontally across the front of a CRT screen

ray tracing

(in graphics) method of creating life-like computer-generated graphics which correctly show shadows and highlights on an object as if coming from a light source; ray tracing software calculates the direction of each ray of light, its reflection and how it looks on an object

RCA connector

see
PHONO CONNECTOR

RDBMS

RELATIONAL DATABASE MANAGEMENT SYSTEM

read only

device or circuit whose stored data cannot be changed

read only attribute

attribute bit of a file that, if set, prevents new data being written to the file or its contents edited

read only memory (ROM)

memory device that has had data written into it at the time of manufacture, and now its contents can only be read
see also
CD-ROM

reader level

(in authoring software) one of two modes that allows a user to run and interact with a multimedia application, but not modify it in any way; the second mode is author level that is used by the developer to design the application

real memory

actual physical memory that can be addressed by a CPU
compare
VIRTUAL MEMORY

real mode

(in an IBM PC) the default operating mode for an IBM PC and the only mode in which DOS operates; real mode normally means a single-tasking operating system in which software can use any available memory or I/O device
compare
PROTECTED MODE

real time

action or processing time which is of the same order of magnitude as the problem to be solved (i.e. the processing time is within the same time as the problem to be solved, so that the result can influence the source of the data)

real-time animation

animation in which objects appear to move at the same speed as they would in real life; real-time animation requires display hardware capable of displaying a sequence with tens of different images every second

real-time video

see
RTV

realize *or* realizing the palette

to select a particular set of colours for a 256-colour palette and use this palette when displaying an image, normally by mapping the colours in a logical palette into the system palette; (in Windows) an application asks Windows to carry out the mapping
see also
LOGICAL PALETTE

recompile

to compile a source program again, usually after changes or debugging

record

to store data or signals on tape or on disk or in a computer

record head *or* write head

transducer that converts an electrical signal into a magnetic field to write the data onto a magnetic medium

recordable CD

see
CD-R

recording density

number of bits of data that can be stored in a unit area on a magnetic disk or tape

recording indicator

light or symbol that shows when a device is recording

recording level

amplification of an input signal before it is recorded; for example, if a voice is very quiet, you can increase the recording level to ensure that it is not degraded by noise

red book audio

see
CD-DA

red, green, blue (RGB)

(i) high-definition monitor system that uses three separate input signals controlling red, green and blue colour picture beams; (ii) the three colour picture beams used in a colour CRT; in a colour TV there are three colour guns producing red, green and blue beams acting on groups of three phosphor dots at each pixel location
compare with
CMYK

reduced instruction set computer (RISC)

CPU design whose instruction set contains a small number of simple fast-executing instructions, that can make program writing more complex, but increases speed of execution of each instruction

reel

circular holder around which a tape is wound

refraction

light or sound that is bent as it travels through a material

refresh

to update regularly the images on a CRT screen by scanning each pixel with a picture beam to make sure the image is still visible

refresh rate

number of times every second that the image on a CRT is redrawn

region fill
to fill an area of a screen or a graphics shape with a particular colour

rehyphenation
changing the hyphenation of words in a text after it has been put into a new page format or line width

relational database management system (RDBMS)
database in which all the items of data can be interconnected; data is retrieved by using one item of data to search for a related field

release
version of a product

rendering
colouring and shading a (normally wire-frame or vector object) graphic object so that it looks solid and real

repetitive strain injury *or* repetitive stress injury (RSI)
pain in the arm felt by someone who performs the same movement many times over a certain period, as when operating a computer terminal

resample
to change the number of pixels used to make up an image; for example, if you scan an image at 400dpi and your printer is only capable of 300 dpi, you could resample the bitmap image to 300dpi, losing some detail but ensuring that what you edit is printed

replay
playing back or reading back data or a signal from a recording

reset
to return a system to its initial state, to allow a program or process to be started again; hard reset is similar to soft reset but with a few important differences: it is a switch that directly signals the CPU, while soft reset signals the operating system; hard reset clears all memory contents, a soft reset does not affect memory contents; hard reset should always reset the system if a soft reset does not always work

reshape handle
(in a GUI) small square displayed on a frame around an object or image that a user can select and drag to change the shape of the frame or graphical object

resolution
(i) number of pixels that a screen or printer can display per unit area; (ii) difference between two levels that can be differentiated in a digitized signal; (iii) degree of accuracy with which something can be measured or timed

resolving power
measurement of the ability of an optical system to detect fine black lines on a white background (given as the number of lines per millimetre)

resonance
situation where a frequency applied to a body, being the same as its natural frequency, causes it to oscillate with a very large amplitude

resource
device or memory or graphic object which can be used by an application or system software

resource allocation
dividing available resources in a system between jobs

resource fork
(in an Apple Macintosh) one of two forks of a file; the resource fork contains the resources that the file needs (fonts, code or icons)

resource interchange file format
see
RIFF

resource sharing
the use of one resource in a network or system by several users

response time
(i) time which passes between the user starting an action (by pressing a key) and the result appearing on the screen; (ii) speed with which a system responds to a stimulus

retention
time taken for a TV image to disappear after it has been displayed, caused by long persistence phosphor

reverb
musical effect that gives the impression of depth in the sound

reverse characters

characters which are displayed in the opposite way to other characters for emphasis (as black on white or white on black, when other characters are the opposite)

reverse video

screen display mode where white and black are reversed (colours are complemented)

rewind

to return a tape or film or counter to its starting point

RF

electromagnetic spectrum that lies between the frequency range 10KHz and 3000GHz

RGB

RED, GREEN, BLUE

(i) high-definition monitor system that uses three separate input signals controlling red, green and blue colour picture beams; (ii) the three colour picture beams used in a colour TV; in a colour CRT there are three colour guns producing red, green and blue beams acting on groups of three phosphor dots at each pixel location

compare with

CMYK

RGB monitor

high-definition monitor system that uses three separate input signals controlling red, green and blue colour picture beams; there are both digital and analogue RGB monitors, both produce a sharper and clearer image than a composite video display; in a colour CRT there are three colour guns producing red, green and blue beams acting on groups of three phosphor dots at each pixel location

ribbon cable

see

TAPE CABLE

rich text format (RTF)

text file format that includes text commands that describe the page, type, font and formatting; the RTF format allows formatted pages to be exchanged between differerent word processing software

RIFF

RESOURCE INTERCHANGE FILE FORMAT
multimedia data format jointly introduced by IBM and Microsoft that uses tags to indentify parts of a multimedia file structure and allow the file to be exchanged between platforms

RIFF chunk

chunk with the ID RIFF

RIFF file

file that contains tagged information that complies with the RIFF file format, such as the WAVE audio file format

right-click menu

pop-up menu that appears when you click on the right-hand button of a two-button mouse; often used to select formatting or the properties of an object

right-hand button

button on the right-hand side of a two or three-button mouse

right justify

printing command that makes the right hand margin of the text evenl the left margin is ragged

RIP

RASTER IMAGE PROCESSOR
computer which translates software instructions into an image or complete page which is then printed by a printer or imagesetter (often used to speed up typesetting images)

RISC

REDUCED INSTRUCTION SET COMPUTER
CPU design whose instruction set contains a small number of simple fast-executing instructions, that makes program writing more complex, but increases speed

RLE

see
RUN LENGTH ENCODING

ROM

READ ONLY MEMORY

ROM cartridge

software stored in a ROM mounted in a cartridge which can easily be plugged into a computer or printer (often used to store extra font data)

root directory

(in a disk filing system) the topmost directory from which all other directories branch; in DOS and OS/2 and Unix this is represented as a single backslash character

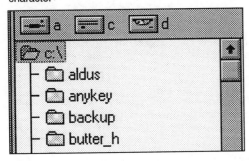

On a PC, the directory structure is below a root directory, shown here at the top of the tree, labelled C:'.

rostrum camera

camera mounted on a stand over a base and used to film artwork or to pan over artwork

rotating helical aperture scanner

type of scanner in which the original image is lit and the reflection sent, through a lens and mirror, through a rotating spiral slit and finally onto a photodetector cell; as the spiral slit turns, it has the effect of moving up the image

rounding characters

making a displayed character more pleasant to look at (within the limits of pixel size) by making sharp corners and edges smooth
see also
ANTI-ALIASING

routine

a number of instructions that perform a particular task, but are not a complete program; they are included as part of a program

row

line of printed or displayed characters

RSI

REPETITIVE STRAIN INJURY *OR* REPETITIVE STRESS INJURY

pain in the arm felt by someone who performs the same movement many times over a certain period, as when operating a computer terminal

RTF

RICH TEXT FORMAT

text file format that includes text commands that describe the page, type, font and formatting; the RTF format allows formatted pages to be exchanged between differerent word processing software

RTV

REAL-TIME VIDEO

real-time video compression used within DVI software to provide usable, but lower-quality, images that are compressed in real-time at 10 frames per second

ruler

bar displayed on screen that indicates a unit of measurement; often used in design, DTP or word-processor software to help with layout

ruler line

line displayed at the top of a document or page, showing the ruler currently in use (including tab stops)

run around

to fit text around an image on a printed page

run length encoding (RLE)

method of compressing image and video data in which it removes a run of pixels of the same value and replaces them with one pixel and a count of the number in the run

run-time

set of library routines required by an application that are called on when it is running; for example, an application developed in Viewer, Toolbook, or Visual Basic requires a number of run-time files supplied by the publisher which carry out various multimedia functions when the program is run

run-time library

library of routines that are stored on disk and are only accessed by an application when it is running and so takes up less memory

run-time licence
licence granted to a user to run an application

run-time version
(i) program code that has been compiled and is in a form that can be directly executed by the computer; (ii) commercial interpreter program that is sold with an application developed in a high-level language that allows it to run

Ss

SAA
SYSTEMS APPLICATION ARCHITECTURE
standard developed by IBM which defines the look and feel of an application regardless of the hardware platform; SAA defines which keystrokes carry out standard functions (such as F1 to display help), the application's display, and how the application interacts with the operating system

sample
measurement of a signal at a point in time

sample and hold circuit
circuit which freezes an analog input signal (using a capacitor) for long enough for an A/D converter to produce a stable output

sample interval
time period between two consecutive samples

sample rate
number of measurements of a signal recorded every second; a PC sound card supports one of the following three standard rates: 11.025, 22.05 and 44.1KHz
see also
ANALOG/DIGITAL CONVERSION; MPC; QUANTIZE

sample size

size of the word used to measure the level of the signal when it is sampled: normally either 8-bit or 16-bit words are used; an 8-bit word means that each sample can have 256 separate levels, a 16-bit word can have 65,536 levels and so is more precise for capturing the finer detail in the signal

sampler

electronic circuit that takes many samples of a signal and stores them for future analysis

saturation

strength of the hue of a colour

SBM

see
SUPER BIT MAPPING

scalable font

method of describing a font which can produce characters in different sizes
see also
OUTLINE FONT

scalar processor architecture

see
SPARC

scan

(i) (optical) to convert a printed image or photograph into a digital bitmap form; (ii) (in a display) to move a picture beam across a screen, one line at a time, to refresh the image on the CRT; (iii) to convert an optical image (from a video camera) into a digital form by examining each pixel on one line of a frame, then moving down one line

scan area

section of an image read by a scanner

scan code

number sequence transmitted from the keyboard to an IBM PC compatible computer to indicate that a key has been pressed and to identify the key

scan conversion

process of converting an interlaced video signal to a non-interlaced signal or a composite to a separated RGB signal

scan head

device used in scanners, photocopiers and fax machines, which uses photo-electric cells to turn an image into a pattern of pixels

scan length

number of items in a file or list that are examined in a scan

scan line

one of the horizontal lines of phosphor (or phosphor dots) on the inside of a CRT or monitor; the monitor's picture beam sweeps along each scan line to create the image on the screen

scanner

(usual term for) a device which uses photo-electric cells to convert an image or drawing or photograph or document into graphical data which can be manipulated by a computer; a scanner is connected and controlled by a computer which can then display or process the image data; a flat-bed scanner is a device with a flat sheet of glass on which the image or photograph or document is placed; the scan head moves below the glass and converts the image into data which can be manipulated by a computer; a hand-held scanner is a device that is held in your hand and contains a row of photo-electric cells which, when moved over an image, convert it into data which can be manipulated by a computer

scan rate

number of times every second that the image on a CRT is redrawn

SCART connector

special connector normally used to carry video or audio signals between video equipment

scissoring

(i) defining an area of an image and then cutting out this part of the image it can then be pasted into another image; (ii) defining an area of an image and deleting any information that is outside this area

scope

range of values that a variable can contain

score

(i) list of actions that control how objects or cast members move with time within a presentation; (ii) description of a piece of music using musical notes

scratchpad memory
cache memory used to buffer data being transferred between a fast processor and a slow I/O device (such as a disk drive)

screen
(i) display device capable of showing a quantity of information, such as a CRT or VDU; (ii) grid of dots or lines placed between the camera and the artwork, which has the effect of dividing the piicture up into small dots, creating an image which can be used for printing

screen angle
angle at which a screen is set before the photograph is taken (different angles are used for the four process colours so as to avoid a moire effect); the normal angles are black: 45°; magenta: 75°; yellow: 90°; cyan: 105°

screen attribute
(in some operating systems, including DOS) attribute bits which define how each character will be displayed on screen; they set background and foreground colours and bold, italic or underline

screen border
margin around text displayed on a screen

screen buffer
temporary storage area for characters or graphics before they are displayed

screen burn
problem caused if a stationary image is displayed for too long on a monitor, burning the phosphor

screen capture
to store the image currently displayed on screen in a file; it is useful when creating manuals about a software product; NOTE: in Windows, you can capture the current screen to the Clipboard by pressing the PrtScrn key, on a Macintosh you can capture the current screen by pressing Shift-Option-3

screen dump
outputting the text or graphics displayed on a screen to a printer

screen flicker
(on a display) image that moves slightly or whose brightness alternates due to a low image refresh rate or signal corruption

screen font

(in a GUI) typeface and size designed to be used to display text on screen rather than be printed out

screen grab

(i) digitizing a single frame from a display or television; (ii) screen capture

screen memory

in a memory-mapped screen, the area of memory representing the whole screen, usually with one byte representing one or several pixels

screen saver

software which, after a pre-determined period of user inactivity, replaces the existing image on screen and displays moving objects to protect against screen burn

screen shot

see
SCREEN CAPTURE

script

set of instructions which carry out a function, normally used with a macro language or batch language

```
Macro2

  Sub MAIN
  num = 628

  EditFind .Find = "#248", .Direction = 0, .MatchCase = 0, .WholeWord
  0, .PatternMatch = 0, .SoundsLike = 0, .Format = 0, .Wrap = 0

  While EditFindFound()
      num = num + 1
      Insert "#" + LTrim$(Str$(num))
      RepeatFind
  Wend

  MsgBox "The word " + Chr$(34) + "success" + Chr$(34) \
      + " occurs" + Str$(num) + " times."

  End Sub
```

Microsoft applications now use the VB-A scripting language.

script channel

(in Movie Player) one channel in a score that contains commands

script editor

editor that lets a user edit a script or program in an authoring package

scripting language

simple programming language (normally proprietary to an application) that allows a user to automate the application's functions; Microsoft applications such as Word and Excel now include a version of Visual Basic as the scripting language

script recorder

function of an authoring package that records the functions and actions a user carries out and converts these into commands in a script

ScriptX™

authoring tool and utilities that allow a developer to write multimedia applications that can be played (unchanged) on a range of different platforms - such as Macintosh and PC; developed by Kaleida Labs, a joint venture between IBM and Apple

scroll

to move displayed text vertically up or down the screen, one line or pixel at a time

scroll arrows

(in a GUI) arrows that when clicked, move the contents of the window up or down or sideways

scroll bar

(in a GUI) bar displayed along the side of a window with a marker which indicates how far you have scrolled

Scroll Lock key

key (on an IBM PC keyboard) that changes how the cursor control keys operate; their function is dependent on the application

SCSI

SMALL COMPUTER SYSTEMS INTERFACE
standard high-speed parallel interface used to connect computers to peripheral devices (such as disk drives and scanners). Fast-SCSI allows data to be transferred at a higher rate than with the original SCSI specification; SCSI-2 is a newer standard that provides a wider data bus and transfers data faster than the original SCSI specification; Wide-SCSI is a development that provides a wider data bus than the original SCSI specification, so can transfer more data at a time; SCSI is the current standard used to interface high-capacity, high-performance disk drives to computers; smaller disk drives are connected with an IDE interface, which is slower, but cheaper. SCSI replaced

the older ESDI interface and allows several (normally eight) peripherals to be connected, in a daisy-chain, to one controller

search
function that allows a user to look through a database or title for a word or phrase

search engine
software that performs the search on a database or title

SECAM
SYSTEME ELECTRONIQUE COULEUR AVEC MEMOIRE
standard for television transmission and reception using a 819-line picture that provides a better image than either PAL or NTSC; SECAM is used in France and eastern Europe

sector
smallest area on a magnetic disk which can be addressed by a computer; the disk is divided into concentric tracks, and each track is divided into sectors which, typically, can store 512 bytes of data

seek
to move to a particular position in a file or on a disk

seek time
time taken by a read/write head to find a particular track on a disk

Sega™
videogame company that develops software and hardware for the console games market; developed the Mega-Drive console

select
(i) to position a pointer over an object (such as a button or menu option) and click on the mouse-button; (ii) to find and retrieve specific information from a database

selection
(in a paint program) to define an area of an image; often used to cut out an area of the image, or to limit a special effect to an area

selection handle
(in a GUI) small square displayed on a frame around a selected area that allows the user to change the shape of the area

selection tool
icon within a toolbar that allows a user to select an area of an image

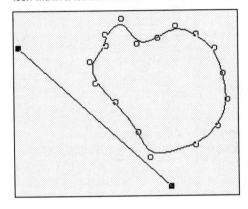

Selection handles are shown here as small squares around two graphic objects; to change the shape or position of an object, the user drags one of the handles.

sensitivity
minimum power of a received signal that is necessary for a receiver to distinguish the signal

sensor glove
glove that fits over a user's hand and has sensors that detect when the user moves his fingers or arm and so control an image on screen; for virtual reality

separation
act of separating a colour image into separate single-colour images (normally four-colour: cyan, magenta, yellow and black) before outputting to film ready to print in four colours on an offset colour printer

sequence
(i) a series of musical notes that define a tune; (ii) a series of video frames

sequencer
(i) software that allows a user to compose tunes for MIDI instruments, record notes from instruments and mix together multiple tracks; (ii) hardware device that can record or playback a sequence of MIDI notes
see also
MIDI SEQUENCER

serial port
connector and circuit used to convert parallel data in a computer to and from a serial form in which each bit is transmitted one at a time over a single wire

server
dedicated computer which provides a function to a network, such as storing images, or printing data

session
(i) one or more instances of an application; (ii) (in a PhotoCD) separate occasion when image data is recorded onto a disc

SGML
STANDARD GENERALIZED MARKUP LANGUAGE
hardware-independent standard which defines how documents should be marked up to indicate bolds, italics, margins and index markers; generally used to code data for database entry or to mark up a book before it is typeset
see also
HTML

shadow mask
sheet with holes placed just behind the front of a colour monitor screen to separate the three-colour picture beams

shareware
software which is available free to sample, but if kept the user is expected to pay a fee to the writer (often confused with public domain software which is completely free)

sheet feed attachment
device which can be attached to a printer to allow single sheets of paper to be fed in automatically

shell
software which operates between the user and the operating system, often to try and make the operating system more friendly or easier to use; for example, MS-DOS's COMMAND.COM is a basic shell that interprets commands typed in at the prompt; the Macintosh Finder is a sophisticated shell with a GUI front-end

shell out
(when running an application) to exit to the operating system whilst the original application is still in memory; the user then returns to the application

shielded cable
cable made up of a conductive core surrounded by an insulator, then a conductive layer to protect the transmitted signal against interference

shoot
to take a picture or record a video sequence with a camera

signal
(i) generated analog or digital waveform used to carry information; (ii) short message used to carry control codes

signal conditioning
converting or translating a signal into a form that is accepted by a device

signal element
smallest basic unit used when transmitting digital data

signal to noise ratio (S/N)
difference between the power of the transmitted signal and the noise on the line

signature
special authentication code, such as a password, which a user gives prior to accessing a system or prior to the execution of a task (to prove his identity)

silicon chip
small piece of silicon in and on the surface of which a complete circuit or logic function has been produced (by depositing other substances or by doping); COMMENT: silicon is used in the electronics industry as a base material for integrated circuits. It is grown as a long crystal which is then sliced into wafers before being etched or treated, producing several hundred chips per wafer. Other materials, such as germanium or gallium arsenide, are also used as a base for ICs

silicon disk or RAM disk
section of RAM made to look and behave like a high speed disk drive

SIMM
SINGLE IN-LINE MEMORY MODULE
small, compact circuit board with an edge connector along one edge that carries densely-packed memory chips, and is used to expand a computer's main memory

simple device
MCI device that does not require a data file for playback, such as a CD drive used to play audio CDs

simulation

operation where a computer is made to imitate a real life situation or a machine, and shows how something works or will work in the future

single in-line memory module

see
SIMM

single in-line package (SIP)

electronic component which has all its leads on one side of its package

single speed

definition of the speed at which a CD-ROM is spun by a drive - normally 230rpm

single-system image

operational view of multiple networks, distributed databases or multiple computer systems as if they were one system

SIP

see
SINGLE IN-LINE PACKAGE

site licence

licence between a software publisher and a user which allows any number of users in one site to use the software

sixteen-bit

(microcomputer system or CPU) which handles data in sixteen bit words, providing much faster operation than older eight-bit systems

skew

the amount by which something which is not correctly aligned

sleep

state of a system that is waiting for a signal (log-on) before doing anything

slide show

feature of a presentation graphics software in which slides (static images) are displayed in a sequence under the control of the presenter

slow scan TV

system used to transmit still video frames over a telephone line

small computer systems interface (SCSI)

standard high-speed parallel interface used to connect computers to peripheral devices (such as disk drives and scanners). Fast-SCSI allows data to be transferred at a higher rate than with the original SCSI specification; SCSI-2 is a newer standard that provides a wider data bus and transfers data faster than the original SCSI specification; Wide-SCSI is a development that provides a wider data bus than the original SCSI specification, so can transfer more data at a time; SCSI is the current standard used to interface high-capacity, high-performance disk drives to computers; smaller disk drives are connected with an IDE interface, which is slower, but cheaper. SCSI replaced the older ESDI interface and allows several (normally eight) peripherals to be connected, in a daisy-chain, to one controller

Smalltalk™

object-oriented programming language developed by Xerox; often used to develop GUI applications

smart terminal

video terminal that is able to process the data it displays; for example, it might be able to provide enhanced display attributes, such as bold and underline

SMPTE

SOCIETY FOR MOTION PICTURE AND TV ENGINEERS
organization that defines standards for television production systems; for example, the SMPTE time code standard is widely used to synchronize audio and video equipment using hours, minutes, seconds, frame data

SMPTE division type

timing format which specifies the number of frames per second used, and in which time is shown as hours, minutes, seconds, frames; standard SMPTE division types are 24, 25 and 30 fps

SMPTE offset

MIDI event that defines when a MIDI file is to be played back

SMPTE time code

method of assigning a unique identifying number to each frame in a video sequence

SMT

see
SURFACE-MOUNT TECHNOLOGY

S/N
see
SIGNAL TO NOISE RATIO

snd
SOUND
(i) in a PC, filename extension used to indicate a file that contains digitized sound data; (ii) in a Macintosh, the resource that contains sound information

snow
interference displayed as flickering white flecks on an monitor

soak
to run a program or device continuously for a period of time to make sure it functions correctly

Society for Motion Picture and TV Engineers
see
SMPTE

software
any program or group of programs which instructs the hardware on how it should perform, including operating systems, word processors and applications programs

software library
number of specially written routines, stored in a library file which can be inserted into a program, saving time and effort

software licence
agreement between a user and a software house, giving details of the rights of the user to use or copy software

software life cycle
period of time when a piece of software exists, from its initial design to the moment when it becomes out of date

software-only video playback
full-motion video standard that can be played back on any multimedia computer, and does not need special hardware - the decompression and display is carried out by software drivers; any software-only standard does not normally provide as sharp an image as a hardware compression system (such as MPEG) or full-screen playback

241

Solaris™
multitasking, multiprocessing operating system and system utilities developed by SunSoft for SPARC computers and PCs with a 80386; Solaris includes the SunOS operating system, similar to Unix, networking products, OpenWindows (a version of X Windows) and the Open Look GUI

solid colour
colour that can be displayed or printed without dithering

solid font printer
printer which uses a whole character shape to print in one movement, such as a daisy wheel printer

solid modelling
(in graphics) function that creates three-dimensional solid-looking objects by shading

song
complete musical tune

song key
musical key used to play a MIDI song

Sony™
electronics company that has developed a wide range of products including the Betamax video system, DataDiscman and camcorder

sound
noise produced by a device, such as a beep or a musical note

sound (snd)
(i) in a PC, filename extension used to indicate a file that contains digitized sound data; (ii) in a Macintosh, the resource that contains sound information

sound bandwidth
range of frequencies that a human ear can register, normally defined as the range from 20Hz to 20KHz

SoundBlaster™
sound card for PC compatibles developed by Creative Labs that allows sounds to be recorded to disk and played back, also includes an FM synthesizer and a MIDI port

sound card

add-on device (usually for a PC) that generates analog sound signals from
digital data, using either a digital-to-analog converter or a FM synthesis chip;
normally also provides functions to record sound in digital form (using an
analog-to-digital converter) and control MIDI instruments; unlike Apple
Macintosh, PC and compatibles do not come with built-in sound generation
hardware, so to produce sound you need to fit a sound card. There are three
major standards for PC sound cards: AdLib, SoundBlaster, and Windows-
compatible; the MPC Level 1 specification states that a sound card should be
able to record sound in 8-bits and sample at 11.025KHz and play back sounds
at 11.025KHz and 22.05KHz; the MPC Level 2 specification states that the
card should be able to record and play sound files: some sound cards provide
built-in compression for wave files, but there are various methods used: the
MPC recommends ADCPM; in addition, many PC sound cards include
electronics to generate sounds from MIDI data on-board: there are two kinds
of MIDI sound generation: FM synthesis simulates musical notes by
modulatng the frequency of a base carrier wave, whereas waveform synthesis
uses digitized samples of the notes to produce a more realistic sound
see also
ADPCM; MIDI; SAMPLE RATE; SAMPLE SIZE

sound file

file stored on disk that contains sound data; this can either be a digitized
analog sound signal or notes for a MIDI instrument

Sound Recorder™

utility included with Microsoft Windows that allows a user to playback digitzed
sound files (the .WAV standard) or record sound onto disk

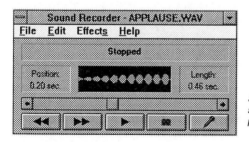

*Sound Recorder utility allows
sound files to be recorded or
played back under Windows.*

sound waves

pressure waves produced by vibrations, which are transmitted through air (or a
solid) and detected by the human ear or a microphone (in which they are
converted to electrical signals)

243

source book

multimedia book from which elements or objects are copied and used in another book

source file

file that contains the data referenced by an OLE object; for example, if you have an OLE object with a link to a spreadsheet, the spreadsheet file is the source file

source object

(in a drag and drop operation) the object that is first clicked on and dragged
see also
DESTINATION OBJECT, DRAG IMAGE

SPARC™

SCALAR PROCESSOR ARCHITECTURE
RISC processor designed by Sun Microsystems which is used in its range of workstations

spatial measurement

method of allowing a computer to determine the position of a pointer within three dimensions (often using a sensitive glove)

speech chip

integrated circuit which generates sounds (usually phonemes) which when played together sound like human speech

speech quality

sound recorded at a low bandwidth with a small sample size; for example, in CD-i it is Level C with 4-bit samples and a rate of 18.9KHz

speech recognition

analysing spoken words in such a way that a computer can recognize spoken words and commands

speech synthesis

production of spoken words by a speech synthesizer

speech synthesizer

device which takes data from a computer and outputs it as spoken words, often by combining a series of phonemes
see also
PHONEME

244

spellcheck

to check the spelling of words in a text by comparing them with a dictionary file

spherization

special effect provided by a computer graphics program that converts an image into a sphere, or 'wraps' the image over a spherical shape

spike

very short duration voltage pulse

splice

to join two lengths of magnetic tape, forming a continuous length

splicing tape

non-magnetic tape which is used to stick together two ends of tape to form a continuous length (the splicing tape is stuck to the back of the magnetic tape so that it does not corrupt the signal)

split screen

software which can divide the display into two or more independent areas, to display two text files or a graph and a text file

spooling

transferring data to a disk from which it can be printed at the normal speed of the printer, leaving the computer available to do something else

sprite

graphic object which moves around in its own plane, independent of other graphic objects on screen; a sprite can normally be given attributes that determine whether it will pass through, over or under any other graphic object which it hits; sprites provide simpler image programming for games and multimedia applications

spurious

unexpected or unwanted data or an error in a signal, often due to noise; the part of the captured signal that is not useful

square wave

pulse that rises vertically, levels off, then drops vertically; the ideal shape for a digital signal

ST

range of personal computers developed by Atari that use the Motorola 68000 series CPU; the ST includes the GEM graphical user interface, sound card, MIDI interface and colour graphics

stack
temporary storage for data, registers or tasks where items are added and retrieved from the same end of the list

stackware
an application developed using the Apple Macintosh HyperCard system

stage window
window in which a video or animation sequence is viewed (normally refers to a window in which a Movie Player sequence is played)

standard colours
range of colours that are available on a particular system and can be shared by all applications; depends on hardware and type of display adapter installed

Standard Generalized Markup Language
see
SGML

standard mode
(in an IBM PC) mode of operation of Microsoft Windows which uses extended memory but does not allow multitasking of DOS applications

startup disk
floppy disk which holds the operating system and system configuration files which can, in case of hard disk failure, be used to boot the computer

startup screen
text or graphics displayed when an application or multimedia book is run; normally displays the product name, logo and copyright information and is only displayed for a few seconds before the main screen appears

statement
line in a program or script that is executed by the compiler or authoring software

static colours
see
SYSTEM COLOURS

static object

object in an animation or video that does not move within the frame

static RAM

RAM which retains data for as long as the power supply is on, and where the data does not have to be refreshed

status bar *or* status line

line at the top or bottom of a screen which gives information about the task currently being worked on (position of cursor, number of lines, filename, time, etc.)

step frame

to capture a video sequence one frame at a time, used when the computer is not powerful or fast enough to capture real-time full-motion video

step through

function of a debugger that allows a developer to execute a program one instruction at a time to see where the fault lies

stereo *or* stereophonic

sound recorded onto two separate channels from two separate microphone elements and played back through a pair of headphones or two speakers; each channel is slightly different to give the impression that the sound is live rather than recorded, and has depth

stick model

see
WIRE FRAME

still

single image or frame within a video or film sequence

story board

series of pictures or drawings on paper that show how a video or animation progresses

streaming

reading data from a storage device in one continuous operation, without processor intervention

string

any series of consecutive alphanumeric characters or words that are manipulated and treated as a single unit by the computer

stroke
(i) the width (in pixels) of the pen or brush used to draw on-screen; (ii) the thickness of a printed character

style
the typeface, font, point size, colour, spacing and margins of text in a formatted document

style sheet
template which can be preformatted to automatically set the style or layout of a document such as a manual, a book, a newsletter, etc. The style sheet includes margins, fonts and type-styles used for different paragraphs

stylus
pen-like device which is used in computer graphics systems to dictate cursor position on the screen

subdirectory
directory of disk or tape contents contained within the main directory

submenu
secondary menu displayed as a choice from a menu; used if there are too many choices to fit into one menu

subroutine
section of a program which performs a required function and can be called upon at any time from inside the main program

subscript
small character which is printed below the line of other characters

suitcase
(in the Apple Macintosh environment) icon which contains a screen font and allows fonts to be easily installed onto the system

suite of programs
(i) group of programs which run one after the other; (ii) number of programs used for a particular task

super bit mapping (SBM)
extension to the Red Book CD-Audio specification in which studio-quality 20-

bit sound samples are stored in the CD-A 16-bit word

supercomputer
very powerful mainframe computer used for high speed mathematical or imaging tasks

super VGA (SVGA)
enhancement to the standard VGA graphics display system which allows resolutions of up to 800x600pixels with 16million colours
see also
>APPENDIX: PC GRAPHICS

super VHS
S-VHS

superscript
small character printed above the normal line of characters

surge
sudden increase in electrical power in a system, due to a fault or noise or component failure

surface-mount technology (SMT)
method of manufacturing circuit boards in which the electronic components are bonded directly onto the surface of the board rather than being inserted into holes and soldered into place

sustain
body of a sound signal
compare with
ATTACK, DECAY

SVGA
SUPER VGA
enhancement to the standard VGA graphics display system which allows resolutions of up to 800x600pixels with 16million colours
>APPENDIX: PC GRAPHICS

S-VHS
SUPER VHS
high-resolution version of the standard VHS video cassette standard which can record 400 lines of a video signal rather than the usual 260 lines of VHS

249

swap

to stop using one program, put it into store temporarily, run another program, and when that is finished, return to the first one

swap file

file stored on the hard disk used as a temporary storage area for data held in RAM, to provide virtual memory
see also
VIRTUAL MEMORY

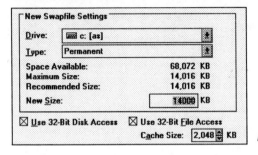

Windows uses a swap file to provide virtual memory.

swim

computer graphics which move slightly due to a faulty display unit

symbol

sign or picture which represents something

sync *or* synchronization

two events or timing signals which happen at the same time

sync bit

transmitted bit used to synchronize devices

sync pulses

transmitted pulses used to make sure that the receiver is synchronized with the transmitter

syntax

grammatical rules which apply to a programming language

synthesized voice

speech created by an electronic device that uses phonemes (the separate sounds that make up speech)

synthesizer

electronic device that generates sounds and music
see also
FM SYNTHESIZER; WAVEFORM SYNTHESIZER

system disk

disk which holds the system software that is used to boot up a computer and load the operating system ready for use

system folder

(in the Apple Macintosh environment) folder that contains the program files for the operating system and Finder

system colours

a palette of 20 colours that are used by Windows for colouring window elements such as borders, captions, buttons

Système Electronique Couleur Avec Mémoire

see
SECAM

system exclusive data

MIDI messages that can only be understood by a MIDI device from a particular manufacturer

system palette

range of colours that are available on a particular operating system and can be shared by all applications; depends on hardware and type of display adapter installed

System 7™

version of the operating system for the Apple Macintosh personal computer that introduced multitasking, virtual memory, QuickTime, and peer-to-peer file sharing

system software

software which makes applications run on hardware

system variable

variable that contains data generated by the system software that can be used by applications; for example, a variable that contains the current time and date, maintained by the computer's real-time clock

Systems Application Architecture (SAA)

standard developed by IBM which defines the look and feel of an application regardless of the hardware platform; SAA defines which keystrokes carry out standard functions (such as F1 to display help), the application's display and how the application interacts with the operating system

Tt

TAB
TABULATE

tab
(i) to tabulate or to arrange text in columns with the cursor automatically running from one column to the next in keyboarding; (ii) in a GUI, method of moving from one button or field to another without using the mouse, but by pressing the tab key to move the focus

tab character
ASCII character 09hex which is used to align text at a preset tab stop

tab key
key on a keyboard, normally positioned on the far left, beside the `Q' key, with two arrows pointing in opposite horizontal directions, used to insert a tab character into text and so align the text at a preset tab stop

tab memory
ability of an editing program (usually a word-processor) to store details about various tab settings

tab rack *or* ruler line
graduated scale, displayed on the screen, showing the position of tabulation columns

tab settings *or* tab stops

preset points along a line, where the printing head or cursor will stop for each tabulation command

tabbing

movement of the cursor in a word-processing program from one tab stop to the next

tabbing order

(in a GUI) order in which the focus moves from one button or field to the next as the user presses the tab key

table of contents

(i) (in a CD) data at the start of the disc that describes how many tracks are on the CD, their position and length; (ii) (in a multimedia title) page with a list of the headings of all the other main pages in the title and links so that a user can move to them

tablet

graphics pad or flat device which allows a user to input graphical information into a computer by drawing on its surface

tabulate

to tabulate or to arrange text in columns with the cursor automatically running from one column to the next in keyboarding

tag

identifying characters attached to a file or item (of data)

tag image file format

see
TIFF

take-up reel

reel onto which magnetic tape is collected

Taligent

operating system developed by IBM and Apple that can be used on both PC and Macintosh platforms

tape

narrow length of thin plastic coated with a magnetic material used to store signals magnetically

tape cable *or* ribbon cable
number of insulated conductors arranged next to each other forming a flat cable

tape cartridge
cassette box containing magnetic tape (on a reel)

tape cassette
small plastic, sealed box containing a reel of magnetic tape and a pickup reel; used in a cassette recorder

Targa™
graphics file format (which uses the .TGA extension on a PC) developed by Truevision to store raster graphic images in 16-, 24- and 32-bit colour; also used to refer to high-resolution colour graphics adapters made by Truevision

target computer
computer on which software is to be run (but not necessarily written on, for example using a cross-assembler)

target disk
disk onto which a file is to be copied

target language
language into which a language will be translated from its source language

target window
window in which text or graphics will be displayed

task swapping *or* switching
exchanging one program in memory for another which is temporarily stored on disk; not the same as multitasking which executes several programs at once

TCP/IP
TRANSMISSION CONTROL PROTOCOL/INTERFACE PROGRAM
data transfer protocol used in networks and communications systems (often uused in Unix-based networks)

TDM
TIME DIVISION MULTIPLEXING
method of combining several signals into one high-speed transmission carrier; each input signal is sampled in turn and the result transmitted, the receiver re-constructs the signals

technical support

(person who provides) technical advice to a user to explain how to use software or hardware or explain why it might not work

telecommuting

practice of working on a computer in one place (normally from home) that is linked by modem to the company's central office allowing messages and data to be transferred

teleconferencing

to link video, audio and computer signals from different locations so that distant people can talk and see each other, as if in a conference room

telesoftware (TSW)

software which is received from a viewdata or teletext service

teletext

method of transmitting text and information with a normal television signal, usually as a serial bit stream which can be displayed using a special decoder

television (TV)

device which can receive (modulated) video signals from a computer or broadcast signals with an aerial, and display moving images on a CRT screen together with sound

television monitor

device able to display signals from a computer without sound, but not broadcast signals (this is usually because there is no demodulator device which is needed for broadcast signals)

television scan

horizontal movement of the picture beam over the screen, producing one line of an image

television tube

CRT with electronic devices which provide the line by line horizontal and vertical scanning movement of the picture beam
see also
CRT, RGB

template

(in text processing) standard text (such as a standard letter or invoice) into which specific details (company address or prices or quantities) can be added

tempo
(i) (in MIDI or music) the speed at which the notes are played, measured in beats per minute (a typical MIDI tempo is 120bpm); (ii) (in a multimedia title) the speed at which frames are displayed

terminal
(i) device usually made up of a display unit and a keyboard which allows entry and display of information when on-line to a central computer system; (ii) an electrical connection point

terminal strip
row of electrical connectors that allow pairs of wires to be electrically connected using a screw-down metal plate

terminate and stay resident (TSR) program
program which loads itself into main memory and carries out a function when activated, normally by a special key sequence or an instruction; used for utilities and for drivers (such as a CD-ROM driver)

terminator
(in a SCSI installation) resistor that fits onto the last SCSI device in the daisy-chain, creating an electrical circuit

text file
stored file on a computer containing text rather than graphics or data

text-to-speech converter
electronic device which uses a speech synthesizer to produce the spoken equivalent of a piece of text that has been entered

texture mapping
(i) special computer graphics effect using algorithms to produce an image that looks like the surface of something (such as marble, brick, stone or water); (ii) to cover one image with another to give the first a texture; for example, if you have an image of a house, you could cover it with an image of a brick and the result is a house filled with a brick pattern

TFT screen
THIN FILM TRANSISTOR SCREEN
method of creating a high-quality LCD display often used in laptop computers
see also
LCD

thermal dye diffusion
method of printing similar to thermal wax transfer, except that a dye is used instead of coloured wax; thermal dye diffusion can print continuous colour to produce a near-photographic output

thermal transfer *or* thermal wax transfer printer
method of printing where the colours are produced by melting coloured wax onto the paper

thesaurus
file which contains synonyms that are displayed as alternatives to a misspelt word during a spell-check

thin film transistor screen
see
TFT SCREEN

thirty-two bit system (32-bit)
microcomputer system or CPU that handles data in thirty-two bit words

thrashing
(i) excessive disk activity; (ii) configuration or program fault in a virtual memory system, that results in a CPU wasting time moving pages of data between main memory and disk or backing store

threshold
preset level which causes an action if a signal exceeds or drops below it; for example, if using a microphone in a noisy environment you might set the threshold high so that only loud noises are recorded

throughput
rate of production by a machine or system, measured as total useful information processed in a set period of time

thumbnail
miniature graphical representation of an image; used as a quick and convenient method of viewing the contents of graphics or DTP files before they are retrieved

TIFF
TAG IMAGE FILE FORMAT
standard file format used to store graphic images (developed by Aldus and Microsoft) that can handle monochrome, grey-scale, 8-bit or 24-bit colour

images; there have been many different versions of TIFF that include several different compression algorithms

tile
(in a GUI) to arrange a group of windows so that they are displayed side by side without overlapping

tilt
to sweep a video camera up and down
compare with
PAN

tilt and swivel
(monitor) which is mounted on a pivoted base so that it can be moved to point in the most convenient direction for the operator

time code
timing information recorded on an audio track in a video tape
see also
SMPTE

time division multiplexing (TDM)
method of combining several signals into one high-speed transmission carrier; each input signal is sampled in turn and the result transmitted, the receiver re-constructs the signals

time out
(of an event or option) to become no longer valid after a period of time

time stamp
(within a MIDI sequence) a MIDI message that is tagged with a time so that a sequencer can play it at the correct moment

tiny model
memory model of the Intel 80x86 processor family that allows a combined total of 64Kb for data and code

title
finished multimedia software product; e.g. an encyclopaedia on a CD-ROM

title bar
horizontal bar at the top of a window which displays the title of the window or application

TMSF time format
TRACKS, MINUTES, SECONDS, FRAMES
MCI time format used mainly by audio CD devices to measure time in frames and tracks

toner
finely powdered ink (usually black) that is used in laser printers; the toner is transferred onto the paper by electrical charge, then fixed permanently to the paper by heating

toner cartridge
plastic container which holds powdered toner for use in a laser printer

tool
(in a graphical front-end) function accessed from an icon in a toolbar, such as a circle-draw option

toolbar
window that contains a range of icons that access tools; for example, paint programs normally have a toolbar that includes icons for colour, brush, circle, text and eraser tools; a floating toolbar is a moveable window that can be positioned anywhere on screen

Toolbook™
multimedia authoring tool developed by Asymetrix, which uses the OpenScript script language to control objects and actions

toolbox
set of predefined routines or functions that are used when writing a program

Toolbox™
(in an Apple Macintosh) set of utility programs stored in ROM that provide graphic functions

toolkit
series of functions which help a programmer write or debug programs

tools
set of utility programs (backup, debugger, format, etc.) in a computer system

touch pad
flat device which can sense where on its surface and when it is touched, used to control a cursor position or switch a device on or off

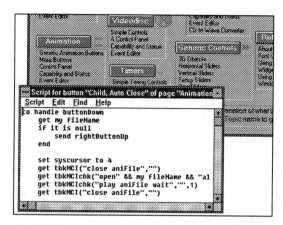

A section of a title developed using *Asymetrix Toolbook authoring software,* the screen is shown behind the script that controls it.

touch screen

computer display which has a grid of infrared transmitters and receivers, positioned on either side of the screen, used to control a cursor position (when a user wants to make a selection or move the cursor, he points to the screen, breaking two of the beams, which gives the position of his finger)

trace

(i) method of verifying that a program is functioning correctly, in which the current status and contents of the registers and variables used are displayed after each instruction step; (ii) (in graphics program) function that can take a bitmap image and process it to find the edges of the shapes and so convert these into a vector line image

trace program

diagnostic program which executes a program that is being debugged, one instruction at a time, displaying the states and registers

trace trap

selective breakpoint where a tracing program stops, allowing registers to be examined

track

(i) (in a music CD) a song; (ii) (in a MIDI file) method of separating the notes within a tune either by channel or by part or instrument; (iii) (in authoring software) series of instructions that define how an object moves with time

trackball

device used to move a cursor on-screen, which is controlled by turning a ball contained in a case with the palm of your hand; rather similar to a mechanical mouse turned up-side down

tracking
(i) correct alignment of a read head and the tape in a tape player; (ii) degradation of a video clip because the action moves too fast to be accurately captured by the camera

tracks, minutes, seconds, frames
see
TMSF

tracing
function of a graphics program that takes a bitmap image and processes it to find the edges of the shapes and so convert these into a vector line image that can be more easily manipulated

transducer
device that can convert a physical action into an electrical signal - for example, a microphone

transfer rate
amount of data that a device can move to another device in a period of time

transient
state or signal which is present for a short period of time

transition
(i) (short) period of time between two events; (ii) period between two frames in a slide show or animation; the user can normally define how one frame changes to the next
see also
WIPE, DISSOLVE, FADE

translate
(i) to convert a program written in one language to a different programming language; for example, you can translate a HyperCard stack into a ToolBook script; (ii) (graphics) to move an image on screen without rotating it

translation tables *or* conversion tables
lookup tables or collection of stored results that can be accessed very rapidly by a process without the need to calculate each result when needed

transparent

(i) graphics object that allows an underlying image to show through (the level of transparency of an object can often be changed in DTP and image processing applications); (ii) computer program which is not obvious to the user or which cannot be seen by the user when it is running

transparency

(i) slide film; (ii) (in graphics) amount one image shows of another image beneath it

transputer

single large very powerful chip containing a 32-bit microprocessor running at around 10 MIPS, that can be connected to other transputer processors to form a parallel processing system (running OCCAM)

trap

device, software or hardware that will catch something, such as a variable, fault or value

trap handler

software that accepts interrupt signals and acts on them (such as running a special routine or sending data to a peripheral)

trashcan

(in a GUI) icon which looks like a dustbin or trashcan; it deletes any file that is dragged onto it

triad

(in a colour monitor) triangular shaped grouping of the red, green and blue colour phosphor spots at each pixel location on the screen of a colour RGB monitor

TrueType™

outline font technology introduced by Apple and Microsoft as a means of printing exactly what is displayed on screen and producing fonts that can be scaled to any point size whilst still being smooth

Tseng Labs™

manufacturer of chipsets used in graphics adapters

TSR

TERMINATE AND STAY RESIDENT (PROGRAM)

TSW
TELESOFTWARE

tuner
electronic circuit that detects a transmitted television carrier signal at a particular frequency and removes the audio or video information to display on a CRT

turtle graphics
graphic images created using a turtle and a series of commands

TWAIN
application programming interface standard developed by Hewlett-Packard, Logitech, Eastman Kodak, Aldus, and Caere that allows software to control image hardware; for example, a paint package can directly control a scanner, scan an image and display the picture

tweening
see
MORPHING

typeface
set of characters in a particular design and particular weight

typesetter
machine which produces very high-quality text output using a laser to create an image on photosensitive paper (normally at a resolution of 1275 or 2450dpi)

type size
size of a font, measured in points

type style
weight and angle of a font, such as bold or italic

Uu

U-Matic™
video tape format, 3/4-inch wide, used for professional video recording; U-Matic SP is an enhanced format of this tape standard that offers better quality

UHF
ULTRA-HIGH FREQUENCY
range of frequencies normally used to transmit television signals

Ultimedia™
multimedia concept developed by IBM that combines sound, video, images, and text, and defines the hardware required to run it

ultra-high frequency
see
UHF

undelete
to restore deleted information or a deleted file

underline *or* underscore
(i) line drawn or printed under a piece of text; (ii) to draw or print a line under a piece of text

ungroup
to convert a single complex object back into a series of separate objects
compare with
GROUP

unique identifier

set of characters used to distinguish between different resources in a multimedia book; each button, image, sound and text is given a unique identifier that allows a programmer to identify and control the object from a program script

Unix

multiuser, multitasking operating system developed by AT&T Bell Laboratories to run on almost any computer, from a PC, to minicomputers and large mainframes; there are a number of graphical user interfaces, such as Open Look, that hide the Unix command-line

upper memory

(in an IBM PC) 384Kb of memory located between the 640Kb and 1Mb limits; upper memory is after the 640Kb conventional memory but before the high memory areas above the 1Mb range

usability

the ease with which hardware or software can be used

user-definable

feature or section of a program that a user can customize as required

user-defined characters

characters which are created by the user and added to the main character set

user-friendly

(language or system or program) which is easy to use and interact with

user interface

software which operates between the user and the operating system, often to try and make the operating system more friendly or easier to use; for example, MS-DOS's COMMAND.COM is a basic shell that interprets commands typed in at the prompt; the Macintosh Finder is a sophisticated shell with a GUI front-end
see also
GUI; SHELL

user level

(in authoring software) one of two modes that allows a user to run and interact with a multimedia application, but not modify it in any way; the second mode is author level that is used by the developer to design, place and create the objects in the application

V20, V30
processor chips made by NEC, which are compatible with the Intel 8088 and 8086

validate
to check that an input or data is correct according to a set of rules

value-added network (VAN)
commercial network which offers information services, such as stock prices, weather, email or advice as well as basic file transfer

value-added reseller (VAR)
company that buys hardware or software and adds another feature, customizes or offers an extra service to attract customers

VAN
VALUE-ADDED NETWORK

vanishing point perspective
graphics displayed in two-dimensions that has the appearance of depth as all lines converge at a vanishing point and objects appear smaller as they are further from the user

vapourware
products which exist in name only

VAR
VALUE-ADDED RESELLER

variable
(in a computer program) identifier for a register or storage location which can contain any number or characters and which may vary during the program run; a global variable contains data that can be accessed by any routine or structure in a program; a local variable contains data which can only be accessed by certain routines or in a certain section of a computer program

Vbox
VIDEO BOX
device that allows several VCRs, videodiscs and camcorders to be attached and controlled by one unit, developed by Sony

VCR
VIDEO CASSETTE RECORDER
machine that can record analog video signals onto a magnetic cassette tape and play-back the tape to display video on a monitor; the most popular formats are: one-inch tape used for studio-quality mastering; 3/4-inch tape was widely used but has now been mostly replaced by 1/2-inch tape; 1/2-inch VHS format tape was first used only in the home but has now mostly replaced 3/4-inch tape; 1/2-inch Beta format tape was the first home VCR format but is no longer used; some VCRs can be used to store digital data for data backup

VDT
VIDEO DISPLAY TERMINAL
see
MONITOR

VDU
VIDEO DISPLAY UNIT
see
MONITOR

vector
coordinate that consists of a magnitude and direction

vector font
shape of characters within a font that are drawn using vector graphics,

allowing the characters to be scaled to almost any size without changing the quality
compare with
BIT-MAPPED FONT

vector graphics *or* vector image *or* vector scan
drawing system which uses line length and direction from an origin to plot lines and so build up an image rather than a description of each pixel, as in a bitmap; a vector image can be easily and accurately re-sized with no loss of detail
compare with
BITMAP IMAGE

vector processor
coprocessor that operates on one row or column of an array at a time

velocity of sound
speed of sound which is equal to 331 metres per second through air; the speed of sound varies in different materials

vendor independent
hardware or software that will work with hardware and software manufactured by other vendors

version
copy or program or statement which is slightly different from others; a newer version of a software product may have new functions or fewer bugs

version control
utility software that allows several programmers to work on a source file and monitors the changes that have been made by each programmer so that each change is reflected in the main file

version number
number of the version of a product

vertical
at right angles to the horizontal

vertical application
application software that has been designed for a specific use, rather than for general use

vertical blanking interval
interval between television frames in which the picture is blanked to enable the picture beam to return to the top left hand corner of the screen

vertical format unit (VFU)
part of the control system of a printer which governs the vertical format of the document to be printed (such as vertical spacing, page length)

vertical interval time code
see
VITC

vertical justification
adjustment of the spacing between lines of text to fit a section of text into a page

vertical scan frequency
number of times a picture beam in a monitor moves from the last line back up to the first

vertical scrolling
displayed text which moves up or down the computer screen one line at a time

vertical sync signal
(in a video signal) signal which indicates the end of the last trace at the bottom of the display

vertical tab
number of lines that should be skipped before printing starts again

VESA
VIDEO ELECTRONICS STANDARDS ASSOCIATION

VESA local bus *or* VL-bus
PC standard defined by VESA which allows up to three special expansion slots that provide direct, bus-master control of the central processor and allow very high speed data transfers between main memory and the expansion card without using the processor; currently, the VL-bus can run at either 40 or 60MHz and support either 32 or 64-bit data transfers

VFU
see
VERTICAL FORMAT UNIT

VFW

See
VIDEO FOR WINDOWS.

VGA

VIDEO GRAPHICS ARRAY
(in an IBM PC) standard of video adapter developed by IBM that can support a display with a resolution up to 640x480 pixels in up to 256 colours; superseded by SVGA which is an enhancement to the standard VGA graphics display system that allows resolutions of up to 800x600pixels with 16 million colours
see
>APPENDIX: PC GRAPHICS

VGA feature connector

26-pin edge connector or port (normally at the top edge) of a VGA display adapter that allows another device to access its palette information and clock signals; often used to provide overlays; for example, a board that displays TV images in a window on screen needs to be synchronized with the VGA adapter

VHS

VIDEO HOME SYSTEM
video cassette tape format, using 1/2-inch wide tape, developed by JVC and now the standard for home and consumer markets
see also
S-VHS

video

text or images or graphics viewed on television or a monitor

video adapter *or* board *or* controller

add-in board which converts data into electrical signals to drive a monitor and display text and graphics

video bandwidth

maximum display resolution, measured in MHz, and calculated by horizontal x vertical resolution x refreshes/sec; TV studio recording is limited to 5MHz; TV broadcasting is limited to 3.58Mhz

video buffer

memory in a video adapter that is used to store the bit-map of the image being displayed

video capture board

high speed digital sampling circuit which stores a TV picture in memory so that it can then be processed by a computer

video cassette recorder

see
VCR

video-CD

CD-ROM that stores digital video data conforming to the Philips White Book standard and uses MPEG compression for the full-motion video data

video codec

electronic device to convert a video signal to or from a digital form
see also
CODEC

video compression

algorithms used to compress analog television signals so that they can be efficiently broadcast over a digital channel

video conferencing

linking two or more computers that can capture and display video and audio in real time so that distant people can talk and see each other, as if in a conference room

video controller

(i) device that allows a computer to control a video recorder or camera; (ii) a video display board

video digitizer

high speed digital sampling circuit which stores a TV picture in memory so that it can then be processed by a computer

videodisc

read-only optical disc that can store up to two hours of video data; normally used either to store a complete film (as a rival to video cassette) or to use in an interactive system with text, video and still images - for interactive use, a videodisc can store 54,000 frames of information. NOTE: if the videodisc contains a complete film, the data is recorded using a constant linear velocity format; if used to store interactive data, it is stored in a constant angular velocity format

video display

device which can display text or graphical information, such as a CRT

video display adapter *or* board *or* card

device which allows information in a computer to be displayed on a CRT (the adapter interfaces with both the computer and CRT); in a digital display adapter (CGA, EGA), the display board generates digital signals for the monitor which then converts from digital to analog, in an analog display system (VGA, Macintosh), the display board creates the analog signals sent to the monitor; NOTE: the monitor must be able to display the frequency range of the adapter or, in the case of multisync monitors, accept the range of frequencies used by the display adapter

video editing

method of editing a video sequence in which the video is digitized and stored in a computer; the editor can then cut and move frames in any order before outputting the finished sequence. The finished sequence can either be recorded directly from the computer output (but this is normally at a lower quality than the original due to compression loss) or the computer can output timecode instructions that can be then used with an editing suite to edit the original video tape

video editor

computer that controls two videotape recorders to allow an operator to play back sequences from one and record these on the second machine; it synchronises the sequences using SMPTE time codes or by counting frames or by using an EDL that has been produced with an off-line editing software package

Video Electronics Standards Association

see
VESA

Video for Windows™ (VFW)

software driver and utilities for Microsoft Windows 3.1, developed by Microsoft, that allows AVI-format video files to be played back in a window; Video for Windows supports several different compression methods including Microsoft Video 1, Microsoft RLE and Intel's Indeo. Once the Video for Windows driver is installed, Video clips can be played back using the Windows Media Player utility; sequences can be edited using the supplied VidEdit utility and video recorded with the VidCap utility; the quality of the video playback depends on the performance of the PC hardware, and the size of the playback window. With a window size of 160x120 pixels, any 486 or higher processor can display flicker-free video; for full-screen video playback at 640x480 pixels only a Pentium-based PC can display smooth motion

A Video for Windows clip normally has an AVI extension and allows a video editing program to manipulate the sound and video playback.

video game
game played on a computer, with action shown on a video display

video graphics array (VGA)
(in an IBM PC) standard of video adapter developed by IBM that can support a display with a resolution up to 640x480 pixels in up to 256 colours, superseded by SVGA which is an enhancement to the standard VGA graphics display system that allows resolutions of up to 800x600pixels with 16 million colours

video graphics card *or* overlay card
expansion card that allows a computer to display both generated text and graphics and moving video images from an external camera or VCR

video home system
see
VHS

video interface chip
chip which controls a video display allowing information stored in a computer (text, graphics) to be displayed

video lookup table
collection of pre-calculated values of the different colours that are stored in

memory and can be examined very quickly to produce an answer without the need to recalculate

video memory *or* video RAM (VRAM)
memory on a video adapter that is used to buffer image data sent from the computer's main memory or to store an image as it is built up

video monitor
device able to display, without sound, signals from a computer

video scanner
device which allows images of objects or pictures to be entered into a computer

video server
dedicated computer on a network used to store video sequences; requires special software or high-speed transmission hardware to ensure smooth playback

video signal
signal which provides line picture information and synchronization pulses with a frequency of between 1- 6MHz

video system control architecture
see
VISCA

video tape recorder (VTR)
machine used to record and playback video signals; the signals are stored on open reels of magnetic tape rather than enclosed cassette used by a VCR

video teleconferencing
linking computers that can capture and display video and so that distant people can talk and see each other, as if in a conference room

videotext *or* videotex
system for transmitting text and displaying it on a screen

video window
window that displays a moving video image, independent of other displayed material
see also
OVERLAY

viewdata

interactive system for transmitting text or graphics from a database to a user's terminal by telephone lines, providing facilities for information retrieval, transactions, education, games and recreation; the user calls up the page of information required, using the telephone and a modem, as opposed to teletext, where the pages of information are repeated one after the other automatically

viewer

utility that allows a user to see what is contained in an image or formatted document file, without having to start the program that created it

Viewer™

multimedia authoring tool for Microsoft Windows and Sony DataDiscman platforms, developed by Microsoft, which uses RTF formatted files with embedded commands

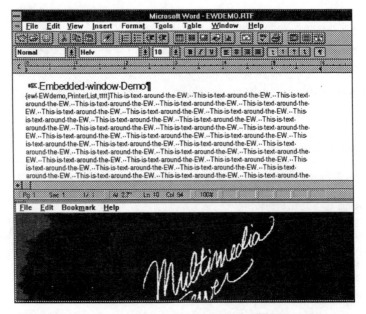

Microsoft Viewer authoring tool; applications are written in RTF files with Word.

virtual address

address that refers to a location in vitual memory

virtual desktop *or* screen

area that is bigger than the physical limits of the monitor, and which can contain text, images, windows, etc; the monitor acts as a window on the virtual screen and can be scrolled around to view a different part of the virtual screen

virtual image

complete image stored in memory rather than the part of it that is displayed

virtual memory

large imaginary main memory made available to an operating system by storing unused parts of the virtual memory on disk and then transferring these pages into available main memory as and when they are required

virtual reality (VR)

simulation of a real-life scene or environment by computer

ViSCA

VIDEO SYSTEM CONTROL ARCHITECTURE
protocol used to synchronize multiple video devices, developed by Sony

Visual Basic™

development product by Microsoft that allows Windows applications to be created quickly and easily without much programming experience by dragging objects onto the design pad and defining how each object works

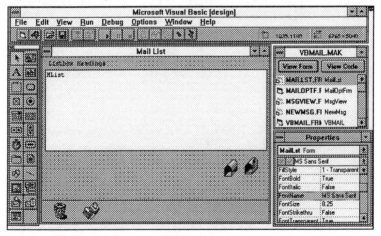

Microsoft Visual Basic development screen; the application being developed is in the centre, with tools around the sides

277

Visual C™

development product by Microsoft that allows Windows applications to be created by drawing the user interface and attaching C code

visualization

conversion of numbers or data into a graphical format that can be more easily understood

visual programming

method of programming a computer by dragging icons into a flowchart that describes the program's actions rather than writing a series of instructions

VITC

VERTICAL INTERVAL TIME CODE

time code recorded onto tape between video frames - preferred to LTC because it doesn't use the audio track and can be read at slow playback speeds

VL-bus *or* VL local bus

VESA LOCAL BUS

PC standard defined by VESA which allows up to three special expansion slots that provide direct, bus-master control of the central processor and allow very high speed data transfers between main memory and the expansion card without using the processor; currently, the VL-bus can run at either 40 or 60MHz and support either 32 or 64-bit data transfers

voice

(i) (in MIDI) another name for a note or sound effect (such as a whistle); instruments that are multi-voice can play several notes at the same time; (ii) sound of a person speaking

voice coil

(i) element in a dynamic microphone which vibrates when sound waves strike it and cause variations in an electrical signal; (ii) element in a loudspeaker that vibrates according to a signal and so produces sound waves

voice response

computer that replies to the user's commands by voice rather than using displayed text

volume

the loudness of a sound or noise

278

VR
VIRTUAL REALITY

VRAM
VIDEO RAM

memory on a video adapter that is used to buffer image data sent from the computer's main memory or to store an image as it is built up

VTR
VIDEOTAPE RECORDER

machine used to record and playback video signals; the signals are stored on open reels of magnetic tape rather than enclosed cassette used by a VCR

wallpaper
(in a GUI) image or pattern used as a background in a window

WAN
WIDE AREA NETWORK
network in which the computers, peripherals and terminals are far apart and are linked by radio, telephone or microwave connections

wand
bar code reader or optical device which is held in the hand to read bar codes on products in a store

Watt
SI unit of measurement of electrical power, defined as power produced when one amp of current flows through a load that has one volt of voltage across it

wave
signal motion which rises and falls periodically as it travels through a medium

WAVE *or* WAV file
standard method of storing an analog signal in digital form under Microsoft Windows (files have the .WAV extension)

waveform

shape of a wave

waveform audio

method of storing analog audio signals as digital data

waveform digitization

conversion and storing a waveform in numerical form normally using an A/D converter

waveform editor

software program that displays a graphical representation of a sound wave and allows a user to edit, adjust levels, frequencies or add special effects

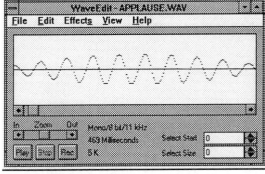

Waveform editor software allows a user to edit a WAVE file.

waveform synthesizer

musical device that creates sounds of an instrument by using recorded samples of the original waveform produced by the instrument
compare with
FM SYNTHESIZER

waveform table

data that describes a sound clip

wavelength

the distance between two adjacent peaks of a wave, equal to the speed divided by the frequency (speed / Hz)

WAV file

see
WAVE

What-You-See-Is-All-You-Get (WYSIAYG)

program where the output on screen cannot be printed out in any other form (that is, it cannot contain hidden print or formatting commands)

What-You-See-Is-What-You-Get (WYSIWYG)

program where the output on the screen is exactly the same as the output on printout, including graphics and special fonts

White Book

formal video-CD standard published by Philips and JVC that defines how digital video can be stored on a CD-ROM; the specification provides 72 minutes of full motion video compressed with the MPEG algorithm

white writer

laser printer which directs its laser beam on the points that are not printed; with a white writer, the black areas are printed evenly but edges and borders are not so sharp

wide area network

WAN

wild card character

symbol used when searching for files or data which represents all files; in DOS, UNIX and PC operating systems, the wild card character `?' will match any single character in this position; the wild card character `or' means match any number of any characters

WIMP

WINDOW, ICON, MOUSE, POINTERS

program display which uses graphics or icons to control the software and make it easier to use; system commands do not have to be typed in; WIMPs normally use a combination of windows, icons and a mouse to control the operating system. In many GUIs, such as Microsoft Windows, Apple Macintosh System 7 and DR-GEM, you can control all the functions of the operating system just by using the mouse. Icons represent programs and files; instead of entering the file name, you select it by moving a pointer with a mouse

window

(i) reserved section of screen used to display special information, that can be selected and looked at at any time and which overwrites information already on the screen; (ii) part of a document currently displayed on a screen; (iii) area of memory or access to a storage device

window, icon, mouse, pointers
see
WIMP

Windows™
multitasking graphical user interface for the IBM PC developed by Microsoft Corp. that is designed to be easy to use; Windows uses icons to represent files and devices and can be controlled using a mouse, unlike MS-DOS which requires commands to be typed in

Windows API
set of standard functions and commands, defined by Microsoft, that allow a programmer to control the Windows operating system from a programming language

Windows GDI
set of standard functions, defined by Microsoft, that allow a programmer to draw images in windows within the Windows operating system

Windows NT™
high-performance GUI derived from Windows that does not use DOS as an operating system and features 32-bit code

Windows SDK™
set of software tools, including definitions of the Windows API, libraries that make it easier for a programmer to write applications that will work under the Windows operating system

Windows for Workgroups™
version of Windows that includes basic peer-to-peer file-sharing functions and email, fax and scheduler utilities

wipe
to clean data from a disk

wire frame model
(in graphics and CAD) objects displayed using lines and arcs rather than filled areas or having the appearance of being solid

word
separate item of data on a computer, formed of a group of bits, stored in a single location in a memory

word wrap *or* wraparound

system in an editing or word processing application in which the operator does not have to indicate the line endings, but can keyboard continuously, leaving the program to insert word breaks and to continue the text on the next line

World Wide Web

WWW

WORM

WRITE ONCE READ MANY TIMES MEMORY

optical disc storage system that allows the user to write data to the disc once, but the user can then read the data from the disc many times

WYSIAYG

WHAT YOU SEE IS ALL YOU GET

WYSIWYG

WHAT YOU SEE IS WHAT YOU GET

The World Wide Web (WWW) graphical interface for the Internet

WWW

WORLD WIDE WEB

(within the Internet) thousands of pages of formatted text and graphics (stored in HTML) that allow a user to have a graphical user interface to the Internet rather than a less user-friendly command-line interface

Xx

X-axis
horizontal axis of a graph

XMS
EXTENDED MEMORY SPECIFICATION
rules that define how a program should access extended memory fitted in a PC

XT
version of the original IBM PC, developed by IBM, that used an 8088 processor and included a hard disk

XT keyboard
keyboard used with the IBM PC which had ten function keys running in two columns along the left-hand side of the keyboard

X-Window System *or* X-Windows
standard set of API commands and display handling routines, that provides a hardware-independent programming interface for applications; originally developed for UNIX workstations, it can also run on a PC or minicomputer terminals

XA
See
CD-ROM XA

Xerox PARC

Xerox development centre that has developed a wide range of important products including the mouse and GUI

XGA

EXTENDED GRAPHICS ARRAY

standard for colour video graphics adapter for PCs, developed by IBM, which has a resolution of 1,024x768 pixels with 256 colours on an interlaced display; XGA-2 provides a resolution of 1024x768 with 64,000 colours

X-Y plotter

device for drawing lines on paper between given coordinates

Y-axis
vertical axis of a graph

Yellow Book
formal specification for CD-ROM published by Philips, includes data storage formats and has an extension to cover the CD-ROM XA standard

YMCK
YELLOW, MAGENTA, CYAN, BLACK
colour definition based on these four colours; used in graphics and DTP software when defining colours or creating separate colour film to use for printing; normally written as CMYK

yoke
electro-magnetic coils around the base of a CRT tube used to control the position of the picture beam

YUV encoding
video encoding system in which the video luminance (Y) signal is recorded at full bandwidth but the chrominance signals (U&V) are recorded at half their bandwidth

Zz

z-axis
axis for depth in a three-dimensional graph or plot

zero fill
to fill a section of memory with zero values

zero insertion force (ZIF) socket
chip socket that has movable connection terminals, allowing the chip to be inserted without using any force, then a small lever is turned to grip the legs of the chip

zero wait state
state of a device (normally a processor or memory chips) that is fast enough to run at the same speed as the other components in a computer, so does not have to be artificially slowed down by inserting wait states

ZIF
see
ZERO INSERTION FORCE SOCKET

zoom
to enlarge an area of text or graphics (to make it easier to see or work on)

APPENDIX A - FILE EXTENSIONS

Extension   Type of file

AD   After Dark image
AFM   Windows Type 1 font metrics
AI   Adobe Illustrator graphics,
      Encapsulated PostScript header
ARC   ARC, ARC+ compressed
ASM   Assembly source code
AVI   Microsoft movie format
BAK   Backup
BAS   BASIC source code
BAT   DOS, OS/2 batch file
BIN   Driver, overlay
BMP   Windows & OS/2 bitmap
C   C source code
CAP   Ventura Pub. captions
CDR   Corel Draw vector graphics
CFG   Configuration
CGM   CGM vector graphics
CHP   Ventura Pub. chapter
CHK   DOS Chkdsk chained file
CIF   Ventura Pub. chapter info.
COB   COBOL source code
CLP   Windows clipboard
COM   Executable program
CPI   DOS code page
CPP   C++ source code
CSV   Comma delimited
CUT   Dr. Halo raster graphics
DAT   Data
DBF   dBASE database
DCA   IBM text
DCT   Dictionary
DIB   Windows DIB raster graphics
DIC   Dictionary
DIF   Spreadsheet
DLL   Dynamic link library
DOC   Document (Multimate, Word...)
DRV   Driver
DRW   Micrografx Designer vector graphics

```
DWG & DXF  AutoCAD vector formats
ED5   EDMICS raster graphics
EPS   Encapsulated PostScript
EXE   Executable program
FLC, FLI  AutoDesk animation
FNT   Windows font
GED   Arts & Letters graphics
GEM   GEM vector graphics
GIF   CompuServe raster graphics
GRF   Micrografx Charisma vector graphics
GRP   Windows ProgMan Group
HLP   Help text
HPL   HP Graphics language
ICO   Windows icon
IMG   GEM Paint raster graphics
INI   Initialization
JPG   JPEG (JFIF) raster graphics
LBM   Deluxe Paint graphics
LIB   Function library
LZH   LHARC compressed
MAC   MacPaint raster graphics
MET   OS/2 Metafile
MEU   Menu items
MDX   dBASE IV multi-index
MID   MIDI sound file
MOV   QuickTime for Windows movie
MSP   Microsoft Paint raster graphics
OBJ   Object module
OVL   Overlay module
OVR   Overlay module
PAS   Pascal source code
PCL   HP LaserJet series
PCD   Photo CD raster graphics
PCM   LaserJet cartridge info.
PCT   PC Paint raster graphics,
      Macintosh PICT raster & vector graphics
PCW   PC Write document
PCX   PC Paintbrush raster graphics
PDF   Printer driver
PDV   PC Paintbrush printer driver
PFA   Type 3 font
PFB   Type 1 font
PFM   Windows Type 1 font metrics
```

```
PGL   HPGL 7475A plotter (vector graphics)
PIC   Vector vector formats:
      Lotus 1-2-3,
      Micrografx Draw,
      Mac PICT format
PIF   Windows info. for DOS programs
PS    PostScript page description
RLE   Compressed (run length encoded)
RTF   Microsoft text/graphics
R8P   LaserJet portrait font
R8L   LaserJet landscape font
SFP   LaserJet portrait font
SFL   LaserJet landscape font
SFS   PCL 5 scalable font
SND   Aristosoft sound
STY   Ventura Pub. style sheet
SYL   SYLK format (spreadsheets)
SYS   DOS, OS/2 driver
TFM   Intellifont font metrics
TGA   TARGA raster graphics
TIF   TIFF raster graphics
TMP   Temporary
TTC   TrueType font compressed
TTF   TrueType font
TXT   ASCII text
USP   LaserJet portrait font
USL   LaserJet landscape font
VOC   Sound Blaster sound
WAV   Windows sound
WMF   Windows Metafile
WPG   WordPerfect raster & vector graphics
ZIP   PKZIP compressed
ZOO   Zoo compressed
$$$   Temporary
```

APPENDIX B - PC DISPLAY MODES

IBM PC Display Standards

```
MDA         720x350 text only, monochrome
Hercules    720x348 text/graphics (mono/non-IBM)
CGA         320x200 text/graphics (4 cols)
EGA         640x350 text/graphics (16 cols)
MCGA        640x400 text-320x200 graphics (256 cols)
VGA         720x400 text-640x480 graphics (16 cols)
8514       1024x768 text/graphics (256 cols)
XGA        1024x768 text/graphics (256 cols)
```

VESA Standards (Super VGA)

```
      640x480 +
      800x600 | text/graphics in 16, 256,
     1024x768 | 32K, 64K and 16M colours
    1280x1024 + (see below)
```

IBM, VESA & Hercules Modes

```
Mode cols    text        Colours
     x rows
```

CGA

```
 0   320x200  40x25 text  16 grey
 1   320x200  40x25 text  16
 2   640x200  80x25 text  16 grey
 3   640x200  80x24 text  16
 4   320x200  graphics    4
 5   320x200  graphics    4 grey
 6   640x200  graphics    2
```

EGA

```
 0   320x350  40x25 text  16 grey
 1   320x350  40x25 text  16
 2   640x350  80x25 text  16 grey
 3   640x350  80x25 text  16
 7   720x350  80x25 text  mono
13   320x200  graphics    16
14   640x200  graphics    16
15   640x350  graphics    2
16   640x350  graphics    16
```

MCGA

```
 0   320x400   40x25 txt   16 grey
 1   320x400   40x25 txt   16
 2   640x400   80x25 txt   16 grey
 3   640x400   80x25 txt   16
17   640x480   graphics    mono
19   320x200   graphics    256
```

VGA

```
 0   360x400   40x25 txt   16 grey
 1   360x400   40x25 txt   16
 2   720x400   80x25 txt   16 grey
 3   720x400   80x25 txt   16
 7   720x400   80x25 txt   mono
18   640x480   graphics    16
```

VESA VBE Standards (Super VGA)

Mode	Resolution	Colors	RAM used
256	640x400	256	250K
257	640x480	256	300K
258	800x600	16	234K
259	800x600	256	469K
260	1024x768	16	384K
261	1024x768	256	768K
262	1280x1024	16	640K
263	1280x1024	256	1280K
264	80x60 text		9.3K
265	132x25 text		6.4K
266	132x43 text		11.1K
267	132x50 text		12.9K
268	132x60 text		15.5K
269	320x200	32K	125K
270	320x200	64K	125K
271	320x200	16M	188K
272	640x480	32K	600K
273	640x480	64K	600K
274	640x480	16M	900K
275	800x600	32K	938K
276	800x600	64K	938K
277	800x600	16M	1406K
278	1024x768	32K	1536K
279	1024x768	64K	1536K
280	1024x768	16M	2304K

281	1280x1024	32K	2560K
282	1280x1024	64K	2560K
283	1280x1024	16M	3840K

Colour Combinations

Number of colors	*Pixel Bits* R	G	B
32K	5	5	5
64K	5	6	5
16M	8	8	8

XGA

640x480	graphics	256 cols
640x480	graphics	64K cols
1024x768	graphics	256 cols

Hercules

720x348	txt/graphics	mono

ASCII IN DECIMAL, HEXADECIMAL

dec.	HEX	CHAR	dec.	HEX	CHAR	dec.	HEX	CHAR	dec.	HEX	CHAR
0	00	NUL	32	20	SP	64	40	@	96	60	
1	01	SOH	33	21	!	65	41	A	97	61	a
2	02	STX	34	22	"	66	42	B	98	62	b
3	03	ETX	35	23	#	67	43	C	99	63	c
4	04	EOT	36	24	$	68	44	D	100	64	d
5	05	ENQ	37	25	%	69	45	E	101	65	e
6	06	ACK	38	26	&	70	46	F	102	66	f
7	07	BEL	39	27	'	71	47	G	103	67	g
8	08	BS	40	28	(	72	48	H	104	68	h
9	09	HT	41	29	)	73	49	I	105	69	i
10	0A	LF	42	2A	*	74	4A	J	106	6A	j
11	0B	VT	43	2B	+	75	4B	K	107	6B	k
12	0C	FF	44	2C	,	76	4C	L	108	6C	l
13	0D	CR	45	2D	-	77	4D	M	109	6D	m
14	0E	SO	46	2E	.	78	4E	N	110	6E	n
15	0F	SI	47	2F	/	79	4F	O	111	6F	o
16	10	DLE	48	30	0	80	50	P	112	70	p
17	11	DC1	49	31	1	81	51	Q	113	71	q
18	12	DC2	50	32	2	82	52	R	114	72	r
19	13	DC3	51	33	3	83	53	S	115	73	s
20	14	DC4	52	34	4	84	54	T	116	74	t
21	15	NAK	53	35	5	85	55	U	117	75	u
22	16	SYN	54	36	6	86	56	V	118	76	v
23	17	ETB	55	37	7	87	57	W	119	77	w
24	18	CAN	56	38	8	88	58	X	120	78	x
25	19	EM	57	39	9	89	59	Y	121	79	y
26	1A	SUB	58	3A	:	90	5A	Z	122	7A	z
27	1B	ESC	59	3B	;	91	5B	[	123	7B	{
28	1C	FS	60	3C	<	92	5C	\	124	7C		
29	1D	GS	61	3D	=	93	5D	]	125	7D	}
30	1E	RS	62	3E	>	94	5E	↑	126	7E	~
31	1F	US	63	3F	?	95	5F	_	127	7F	DEL

THE ASCII SYMBOLS

NUL	*Null*		DLE	*Data Link Escape*
SOH	*Start of Heading*		DC	*Device Control*
STX	*Start of Text*		NAK	*Negative Acknowledge*
ETX	*End of Text*		SYN	*Synchronous Idle*
EOT	*End of Transmission*		ETB	*End of Transmission Block*
ENQ	*Enquiry*		CAN	*Cancel*
ACK	*Acknowledge*		EM	*End of Medium*
BEL	*Bell*		SUB	*Substitute*
BS	*Backspace*		ESC	*Escape*
HT	*Horizontal Tabulation*		FS	*File Separator*
LF	*Line Feed*		GS	*Group Separator*
VT	*Vertical Tabulation*		RS	*Record Separator*
FF	*Form Feed*		US	*Unit Separator*
CR	*Carriage Return*		SP	*Space (Blank)*
SO	*Shift Out*		DEL	*Delete*
SI	*Shift In*			

I want to order/Please send me details of:

Mail or fax to: 1 Cambridge Road, Teddington, TW11 8DT, UK (fax 0181 943 1673)

English

Accounting	0-948549-27-0	❏
Agriculture, 2nd ed	0-948549-78-5	❏
American Business	0-948549-11-4	❏
Automobile Eng.	0-948549-66-1	❏
Banking & Finance	0-948549-12-2	❏
Business, 2nd ed	0-948549-51-3	❏
Computing, 2nd ed.	0-948549-44-0	❏
Vocabulary for Computing	0-948549-58-0	❏
Ecology & Environment, 3rd	0-948549-74-2	❏
Goverment & Politics	0-948549-05-X	❏
Hotels, Tourism & Catering	0-948549-40-8	❏
Information Technology	0-948549-03-3	❏
Law, 2nd ed	0-948549-33-5	❏
Library & Information Mgmt	0-948549-68-8	❏
Marketing	0-948549-08-4	❏
Medicine, 2nd ed	0-948549-36-X	❏
Multimedia	0-948549-69-6	❏
Personnel Management,2e	0-948549-79-3	❏
Printing & Publishing	0-948549-09-2	❏
Science & Technology	0-948549-67-X	❏

English-French/French-English

Business, 2nd ed	0-948549-64-5	❏
Computing, 2nd ed	0-948549-65-3	❏
Ecology & Environment	0-948549-29-7	❏

English-Swedish/Swedish-English

Business (hb)	0-948549-14-9	❏
Computing/IT (hb)	0-948549-16-5	❏
Law (hb)	0-948549-15-7	❏
Medicine (hb)	0-948549-23-8	❏

English-German/German-English

Agriculture (hb)	0-948549-25-4	❏
Banking & Finance (hb)	0-948549-35-1	❏
Business new edn. (hb)	0-948549-50-5	❏
Computing/IT (hb)	0-948549-20-3	❏
Ecology (hb)	0-948549-21-1	❏
Law (hb)	0-948549-18-1	❏
Marketing (hb)	0-948549-22-X	❏
Medicine (hb)	0-948549-26-2	❏
Print/Publishing (hb)	0-948549-19-X	❏

English-Spanish/Spanish-English

Business (hardback)	0-948549-30-0	❏

English-Chinese

Business (hb)	0-948549-63-7	❏

Name: . . . .

Address: . . . .

. . . . Postcode: . . . .